TExES Principal
068 Teacher Certification Exam

By: Sharon A. Wynne, M.S.

XAMonline, Inc.
Boston

XAMonline, Inc.
21 Orient Avenue
Melrose, MA 02176
Toll Free 1-800-301-4647
Email: info@xamonline.com
Web www.xamonline.com

Library of Congress Cataloging-in-Publication Data
Wynne, Sharon A.

    TExES Principal (068): Teacher Certification / Sharon A. Wynne.
    ISBN 978-1-60787-738-7

1. Principal   2. Study Guides.   3. TExES
4. Teachers' Certification & Licensure.   5. Careers

Disclaimer:
The opinions expressed in this publication are the sole works of XAMonline and were created independently from the National Education Association, Educational Testing Service, or any State Department of Education, National Evaluation Systems or other testing affiliates.

Between the time of publication and printing, state specific standards as well as testing formats and website information may change that is not included in part or in whole within this product. XAMonline developed the sample test questions and the questions reflect similar content as on real tests; however, they are not former tests. XAMonline assembles content that aligns with state standards but makes no claims nor guarantees teacher candidates a passing score. Numerical scores are determined by testing companies such as NES or ETS and then are compared with individual state standards. A passing score varies from state to state.

Printed in the United States of America
TExES: Principal (068)
ISBN: 978-1-60787-738-7

TExES™ Principal
Test at a Glance

Time	5 Hours
Number of Questions	115 multiple-choice questions
Format	Paper-based test (PBT) Computer-administered test (CAT)

Domain	Domain Title	Approx. Percentage of Test
I.	School Community Leadership	33%
II.	Instructional Leadership	45%
III.	Administrative Leadership	22%

About This Test

The TExES Principal (068) test is designed to assess whether an examinee has the requisite knowledge and skills that an entry-level educator in this field in Texas public schools must possess. The 115 multiple-choice questions are based on the Principal test framework. Questions on this test range from grades EC–12. The test may contain questions that do not count toward the score.

The Test Framework

The content covered by the test is organized into broad areas of content called domains. Within each domain, the content is further defined by a set of competencies. Each competency is composed of two major parts:

> The **competency statements**, which broadly define what an entry-level educator in this field in Texas public schools should know and be able to do.

> The **descriptive statements**, which describe in greater detail the knowledge and skills eligible for testing.

The following is a complete set of the framework's competencies and descriptive statements. Read each competency with its descriptive statements to get a more specific idea of the knowledge you will be required to demonstrate on the test.

Table of Contents

time for round table discussions

11 activities & strategies that work for him

* *School community* includes students, staff, parents/caregivers, and community members.

COMPETENCY 2.0 THE PRINCIPAL KNOWS HOW TO COMMUNICATE AND COLLABORATE WITH ALL MEMBERS OF THE SCHOOL COMMUNITY, RESPOND TO DIVERSE INTERESTS AND NEEDS, AND MOBILIZE RESOURCES TO PROMOTE STUDENT SUCCESS.

DOMAIN II.   INSTRUCTIONAL LEADERSHIP

COMPETENCY 4.0 THE PRINCIPAL KNOWS HOW TO FACILITATE THE DESIGN AND IMPLEMENTATION OF CURRICULA AND STRATEGIC PLANS THAT ENHANCE TEACHING AND LEARNING; ENSURE ALIGNMENT OF CURRICULUM, INSTRUCTION, RESOURCES, AND ASSESSMENT; AND PROMOTE THE USE OF VARIED ASSESSMENTS TO MEASURE STUDENT PERFORMANCE.

[handwritten: TEKS]
[handwritten: goals + objectives]
[handwritten: campus improvement plan]

COMPETENCY 5.0 THE PRINCIPAL KNOWS HOW TO ADVOCATED, NURTURE, AND SUSTAIN AN INSTRUCTIONAL PROGRAM AND A CAMPUS CULTURE THAT ARE CONDUCIVE TO STUDENT LEARNING AND STAFF PROFESSIONAL GROWTH.

COMPETENCY 7.0 THE PRINCIPAL KNOWS HOW TO APPLY ORGANIZATIONAL, DECISION-MAKING, AND PROBLEM-SOLVING SKILLS TO ENSURE AN EFFECTIVE LEARNING ENVIRONMENT.

DOMAIN III.   **ADMINISTRATIVE LEADERSHIP**

COMPETENCY 8.0 THE PRINCIPAL KNOWS HOW TO APPLY PRINCIPLES OF EFFECTIVE LEADERSHIP AND MANAGEMENT IN RELATION TO CAMPUS BUDGETING, PERSONNEL, RESOURCE UTILIZATION, FINANCIAL MANAGEMENT, AND TECHNOLOGY USE.

COMPETENCY 9.0 THE PRINCIPAL KNOWS HOW TO APPLY PRINCIPLES OF LEADERSHIP AND MANAGEMENT TO THE CAMPUS PHYSICAL PLANT AND SUPPORT SYSTEMS TO ENSURE A SAFE AND EFFECTIVE LEARNING ENVIRONMENT.

remodeling school
• takes into consideration

* notify only those that need to know *

• exemption from immunizations
* - military*
* - religious - parent*
* - allergy - doc*

prevention - mitigation

Great Study and Testing Tips!

What to study to prepare for the subject assessments is the focus of this study guide, but equally important is *how* you study.

You can increase your chances of mastering the information by taking some simple but effective steps.

Study Tips:

1. Some foods aid the learning process. Foods such as milk, nuts, seeds, rice, and oats help your study efforts by releasing natural memory enhancers called CCKs (*cholecystokinin*) composed of *tryptophan*, *choline*, and *phenylalanine*. All of these chemicals enhance the neurotransmitters associated with memory. Before studying, try a light, protein-rich meal of eggs, turkey, and fish. All of these foods release the memory-enhancing chemicals. The better the connections, the more you comprehend.

Likewise, before you take a test, stick to a light snack of energy-boosting and relaxing foods. A glass of milk, a piece of fruit, or some peanuts all release various memory-boosting chemicals and help you relax and focus on the subject at hand.

2. Learn to take great notes. A byproduct of our modern culture is that we have grown accustomed to getting our information in short doses (i.e., TV news sound bites or *USA Today*–style newspaper articles).

Consequently, we've subconsciously trained ourselves to assimilate information better in neat little packages. If your notes are scrawled all over the paper, it fragments the flow of the information. Strive for clarity. Newspapers use a standard format to achieve clarity. You can make your notes much clearer by using proper formatting. A very effective format is called the *Cornell Method.*

> Take a sheet of loose-leaf lined notebook paper and draw a line all the way down the paper, about 1–2" from the left edge.
>
> Draw another line across the width of the paper, about 1–2" from the bottom. Repeat this process on the reverse side of the page.

Look at the effective result. You have ample room for notes, a left-hand margin for special emphasis items or supplementary data from the textbook, a large area at the bottom for a brief summary, and a little rectangular space for anything you want.

3. Get the concept, then the details. Too often we focus on the details without understanding the concept. If you simply memorize dates, places, or names, you may well miss the whole point of the subject.

A key way to understand things is to put them in your own words. If you are working from a textbook, summarize each paragraph in your mind. If you are outlining text, don't simply copy the author's words. *Rephrase* them in your own words. You remember your own thoughts and words much better than someone else's, and you subconsciously tend to associate the important details with the core concepts.

4. Ask *Why?* Pull apart written material paragraph by paragraph and don't forget the captions under the illustrations.

Example: If the heading is Stream Erosion, flip it around to read, "Why do streams erode?" Then answer the question.

If you train your mind to think in a series of questions and answers, you will not only learn more but also experience less test anxiety because you are used to answering questions.

5. Read for reinforcement and future needs. Even if you only have 10 minutes, put your notes or a book in your hand. Your mind is similar to a computer; you have to input data to have it processed. *By reading, you are creating the neural connections for future retrieval.* The more times you read something, the more you reinforce the learning of ideas.

Even if you don't fully understand something on the first pass, *your mind stores much of the material for later recall.*

6. Relax to learn, so go into exile. Our bodies respond to an inner clock called biorhythms. Burning the midnight oil works well for some people, but not everyone.

If possible, set aside a particular place to study that is free of distractions. Shut off your television and cell phone and exile your friends and family during your study period.

If you really are bothered by silence, try background music. Light classical music at a low volume has been shown to aid in concentration more than other types of music. Music that evokes pleasant emotions without lyrics is highly suggested. Try just about anything by Mozart. It relaxes you.

7. <u>Use arrows, not highlighters</u>. At best, it's difficult to read a page full of yellow, pink, blue, and green streaks. Try staring at a neon sign for a while—you'll see that the horde of colors obscures the message.

A quick note, a brief dash of color, an underline, and an arrow pointing to a particular passage is much clearer than a horde of highlighted words.

8. <u>Budget your study time</u>. Although you shouldn't ignore any of the material, *allocate your available study time in the same ratio that topics may appear on the test.*

Testing Tips:

1. Get smart, play dumb. Don't read anything into the question. Don't make an assumption that the test writer is looking for something else than what is asked. Stick to the question as written and don't read extra things into it.

2. Read the question and all the answer choices *twice* before answering the question. You may miss something by not carefully reading and then rereading both the question and the answers.

If you really don't know the right answer, leave it blank on the first time through. Go on to the other questions, as they may provide a clue about the answer to the skipped question.

If, later, you still can't answer the skipped questions, *guess.* The only risk of guessing is that you *might* get the question wrong. One thing is certain—if you don't answer the question, you *will* get it wrong!

3. Turn the question into a statement. Look at the way the questions are worded. The syntax of the question usually provides a clue. Does it seem more familiar as a statement than as a question? Does it sound strange?

By turning a question into a statement, you may be able to spot if an answer sounds right, and this also may trigger memories of material you have read.

4. Look for hidden clues. It's actually very difficult to compose multiple-foil (choice) questions without giving away part of the answer in the options presented.

In many multiple-choice questions, you can readily eliminate one or two of the potential answers. This leaves you with only two possibilities, so your chances of answering the question correctly are 50-50.

5. Trust your instincts. For every fact that you have read, you subconsciously retain something of that knowledge. On questions about which you aren't certain, go with your instincts. **Your first impression on how to answer a question is usually correct.**

6. Mark your answers directly on the test booklet. Don't bother trying to fill in the optical scan sheet on the first pass through the test.

Be very careful not to mismark your answers when you transcribe them to the scan sheet.

7. Watch the clock! You have a set amount of time to answer the questions. Don't get bogged down trying to answer a single question at the expense of 10 questions you can more readily answer.

DOMAIN I.   SCHOOL COMMUNITY LEADERSHIP

COMPETENCY 1.0 THE PRINCIPAL KNOWS HOW TO SHAPE CAMPUS CULTURE BY FACILITATING THE DEVELOPMENT, ARTICULATION, IMPLEMENTATION, AND STEWARDSHIP OF A VISION OF LEARNING THAT IS SHARED AND SUPPORTED BY THE SCHOOL COMMUNITY.

Skill 1.1   Create a campus culture that sets high expectations, promotes learning, and provides intellectual stimulation for self, students, and staff.

One of the most important jobs of an instructional leader is to change the prevailing culture of a school. Roland Barth wrote that "a school's culture has far more influence on life and learning in the schoolhouse than the president of the country, the state department of education, the superintendent, the school board, or even the principal, teachers, and parents can ever have."

Principals are charged with leaving "no child behind," and this involves a fundamental change in the culture of the school. It is no longer acceptable for the majority of students to do well. Educators now are required to ensure high levels of learning for all students. Today's school leaders must lead the staff and community in efforts to close the achievement gap between high and low performers, develop students' thinking and problem-solving skills, and attend to students' social and emotional development.

School leaders must articulate and implement a vision of learning and ensure that it is shared by the school community. Leadership to create a campus culture of high expectations requires a sense of urgency and a mix of pressure and support. If a principal is assigned to lead a school in which many students are struggling, that principal needs to fast track the change by pushing hard on standards, delivering quality support material and examples of successful practice, and providing focused professional development. As student achievement increases, the principal should shift to capacity building to encourage local ownership. Leaders should strive to move from tighter to looser control and from external control to internal commitment.

Michael Fullan has written about the culture of dependency among schools—the tendency to wait for solutions from outside. Any kind of improvement is a function of learning to do the right thing in the setting in which you work. Ultimately no amount of outside motivation can specify the best solutions for a particular situation. Principals who help their schools form professional learning communities (PLCs) embrace the notion that the primary purpose of a school is learning, not just teaching. Educators in PLCs examine the practices of their schools to find ways to ensure that all children will learn. Professional learning communities continuously examine what is worthwhile and how to get there.

- School staff members must work together to figure out what is needed to achieve the goal of "no child left behind."
- Internal commitment and ingenuity does not come from outside the school; expertise lies within.
- Change is forever. Problems don't stay solved, so you have to keep learning to do the right thing.

Schools that establish high expectations for all students . . . and provide the support necessary to achieve these expectations . . . have high rates of academic success (Brook et al., 1989; Edmonds, 1986; Howard, 1990; Levin, 1988; Rutter et al., 1979; Slavin et al., 1989). Successful schools share certain characteristics: an emphasis on academics, clear expectations and regulations, high levels of student participation, and alternative resources such as library facilities, vocational work opportunities, art, music, and extracurricular activities. Conveying positive and high expectations to students occurs in several ways. One of the most obvious and powerful is through personal relationships in which teachers and other school staff communicate to students that "this work is important; I know you can do it; I won't give up on you" (Howard, 1990). Successful teachers look for children's strengths and interests and use these as starting points for learning. A relationship that conveys high expectations to students can internalize these beliefs in students and develop self-esteem and self-efficacy.

Skill 1.2   Ensure that parents and other members of the community are an integral part of the campus culture.

All parents have deeply personal reasons to support the school's efforts: they want their children to do well in school. Some parents will have strong opinions about how the principal should run a school; if they were star students, they may want the principal to replicate their school experiences. But many parents have memories of their own schooling that are less positive, and these memories hamper their involvement in the school. Principals must constantly communicate the school's vision so that parents understand what the school is trying to accomplish. Uninformed parents and community members can derail your improvement efforts.

Educating the parents and community about the school's programs, goals, and results is a key responsibility of the school principal, but such communication will be different for every school building and school community. Your parents are as diverse as your student population, with varying degrees of understanding and prior knowledge. Communicating in a variety of ways will enable you to reach your goals of parent and community involvement. Fullan writes about the power of three: teachers, parents, and students working together. Parental involvement is a force for school improvement that we must tap.

Successful principals share leadership as they reach out to their parents and community, and they work hard to develop a coherent professional community. Effective leaders are energy creators: creating harmony, forging consensus, setting high standards, and developing a "try this" future orientation. They are forever hopeful and cause everyone in the school's community to share this hope.

See Skills 2.1, 2.3, and 2.5 for more ideas on parent and community involvement.

Skill 1.3   Implement strategies to ensure the development of collegial relationships and effective collaboration.

"Quality teaching requires strong professional learning communities. Collegial interchange, not isolation, must become the norm for teachers. Communities of learning can no longer be considered utopian; they must become the building blocks that establish a new foundation for America's school."

—National Commission on Teaching, 2003, p. 17

Teaching quality and levels of learning will both improve when a simple, powerful structure is used. It starts with a group of teachers who meet regularly as a team to identify essential and valued student learning, develop common formative assessments, analyze current levels of achievement, set achievement goals, and then share and create lessons to improve upon those levels.

These teams of teachers implement these new lessons, continuously assessing their results and then adjusting their lessons in light of those results. Importantly, there must be an expectation that this collaborative effort will produce ongoing improvement and gains in achievement.

Professional learning communities are schools in which teachers and leaders work together and focus on student learning. All educational change depends on what teachers do and think—yet the conditions for teaching appear to have deteriorated. Stress, alienation, and the intense nature of the teacher's work are at an all-time high. Newly imposed curriculum standards and accountability demands leave teachers working in isolation and increasingly feeling frustrated and burnt out. Collegiality provides the best starting point in the process of teacher regeneration. Teaching needs to be seen as a collective rather than an individual enterprise. Successful schools, using the model of professional learning communities, develop the capacity to self-reflect, to examine student performance, and to act on their own understandings.

What passes for collaboration or collegiality in many schools lacks a focus on achievement results—on short-term, formative assessment—and thus has little impact on the character and quality of teaching. When teachers engage regularly in authentic joint work focused on explicit, common learning goals, their collaboration pays off richly in the form of higher-quality solutions to instructional problems, increased teacher confidence, and remarkable gains in achievement. Discussions about curricular issues or popular strategies can feel good but go nowhere. Principals must set aside the time for groups of teachers to meet regularly to share, refine, and assess the impact of lessons and strategies to help increasing numbers of students learn at higher levels. By establishing times before, after, and during the school day for such collaboration, principals can eliminate isolated practice and make these planning sessions a priority. Sometimes, substitute teachers can be used to give teachers additional planning time. Principals should join these groups, not as the leader, but as a study partner, assisting in the discussion about what is working and what is not, based on student data analysis.

Skill 1.4   Respond appropriately to diverse needs in shaping the campus culture.

Education is both a public and a private good because it enhances the individual as it brings important benefits to society (Swanson and King, 1997). At an individual level, education provides the ability to enjoy a higher standard of living by earning more money and living a better quality of life, thus making a contribution to the economy. Education supports the production of a skilled workforce for the efficient functioning of a society that is stimulated by economic growth and development.

Schools operate in an open system model, in which external influences impact the effectiveness of the school-based administration and leadership. External influences provide input into the system of schooling in the form of people, policies, values, laws, technology, and other material resources. This input directly or indirectly affects not only school business decisions, such as finance and purchasing, but also other functions of school operation, such as the curriculum and pupil services.

It does not matter how efficient and knowledgeable the school-based administrator might be in the endeavors of managing the school if there is a lack of clear understanding of the community's power structures, its strengths, and its effects on the operation of the school. Nudge, Anthony, and Gayles (1996) suggest that understanding how power is distributed both internally and externally and understanding the political nature of organizations are two crucial components to better understand the actions or inactions of organizations. To better understand the political nature of the school organization, administrators must understand the difference between authority and power. Legal-rational organizations base their authority on formal policies and vest authority of command in specific individuals. Power, in contrast, is the capacity to control or influence the behaviors of others (Hansen, 1996).

School administrators must be aware of the various dimensions of educational politics in school districts—politics of the community, politics of the state and the federal government, politics of the profession, politics of the local board of education, and politics of the bureaucracy (Kimbrough and Nunnery, 1988). Perhaps the most important politics for school-based administrators are the politics of the community and its power structure. The school organizational structure is greatly affected by existing conditions in the local community such as customs, traditions, and value systems. These conditions affect the power that is exercised on the formal and informal decision-making process at the school district and school building levels. The biggest challenge is to identify the main power brokers in the community and learn how to work with them.

Additionally, practicing administrators must understand the politics involved in the process of educational policy development at the state and district levels. The increase in government funding for education has paralleled the interest of educators in the nature of laws being considered or passed and policy development at the federal, state, and local levels. Mandates and policies have direct implications for school-level implementation of programs to meet the needs of children, especially when the level of funding is incongruent with the requirements of the law. State politicians constantly struggle to reduce federal involvement in programs and return more control to state government, at times losing sight of the fact that the goal of the federal government's participation is the constitutional mandate of equalizing funding to provide an equal education for all children

School administration has evolved into an inclusive and cooperative endeavor with a structure that endorses a participatory model to include not only administrators and teachers, but also parents, business partners, and other interested citizens in the community. Therefore, the planning process must be ongoing and systematic to allow time for the development of unity of purpose, methodology, and desirable outcome.

Planning must be continuous at both the district and the school building levels, even though the process used at one level may overlap with the other.

The rational approach to planning follows a logical sequence to accomplish organizational goals. It begins with setting goals, which includes articulating the mission of the organization and clarifying specific goals to be attained. The action plan is the implementation tool, and it must have two components: a long-term plan that includes general projections and a short-term plan that includes the details to carry out the actions deemed necessary. The evaluation process provides feedback for improvement. After evaluation, the process is repeated. Although useful to school administrators, the rational approach provides only general principles that are applicable to many areas of planning.

The evaluation component that is built into the process not only assesses the effectiveness of the goal, but also measures the level of goal attainment over specific periods of time.

Skill 1.5 **Use various types of information (e.g., demographic data, campus climate inventory results, student achievement data, emerging issues affecting education) to develop a campus vision and create a plan for implementing the vision.**

All leaders must have the capacity to plan. The ability to plan is an essential skill in today's high pressure and ever-changing school environment. It helps administrators organize their work and project solutions to problems. Determining about what to plan for precedes the activity of planning.

Schools need to plan the curriculum, to plan for students, and to plan for teachers. Planning needs emerge from problems in the environment that are identified and defined. Planning is attached to goals and objectives. Who participates in the planning process is crucial to receiving a quality and dynamic plan for implementation.

Planning begins with the identification of a need—a measurable discrepancy between what currently exists and a desired outcome. It is common for a decision-maker to act before thinking. Planning is a commitment to think before acting. This prevents administrators from being embroiled in a set of negative consequences. Planning can be defined as a conceptualization of activities to reach an objective. Planning has anticipated and unanticipated consequences. Planning, like decision making, often occurs without all the necessary information. Critics of the current drive for "strategic planning" argue that too much attention on planning blinds school personnel from accomplishing their plans. However, no planning is worse than poor planning.

Plans develop from the process of planning and entail an agreement on long-term and short-term goals that move the school from where it is to where stakeholders want it to be (Kaiser, 1996). Schools need to have a strategic plan that details what the school wants to accomplish over a period of time.

Administrators engage in the planning process as a means of accomplishing desired objectives and accommodating future events that can impact the school positively or negatively. Schools, being open systems, are dependent on their external environment and are subject to the uncertainties that exist in that environment. As part of planning, administrators can identify both potential support to accomplish school goals and elements that can have a negative influence on the functioning of the school.

Principals know that student achievement data offers invaluable support for making good decisions about instruction. But how that data are used is critical. To help all students achieve, teachers need to systematically and routinely use data to guide instructional decisions and meet students' learning needs. To gain a deeper understanding of students' learning needs, teachers need to collect data from multiple sources, such as annual state assessments, interim district and school assessments, classroom performance, and other relevant sources.

A district-wide data system allows teachers to aggregate data by classroom, content area, or assignment type to identify patterns in performance. While developing a written plan that ties data use to a school's goals, a data team should ensure that goals are attainable, measurable, and relevant. The written plan needs to be actionable and include critical elements such as specific data use activities, staff roles and responsibilities, and timelines. This could be a component incorporated into the school's strategic plan for student achievement or any other existing plans for various funding sources such as Title I, literacy, and so on.

Skill 1.6 Use strategies for involving all stakeholders in planning processes to enable the collaborative development of a shared campus vision focused on teaching and learning.

Planning is a key factor in getting the work of a school done. Mandates from superiors, desires of subordinates or others in the learning community, and the school's vision are a few of the reasons that planning is critical. In designing a plan, the school leader must establish deadlines, develop a flow of activities, identify resource allocations, and ascertain evaluation strategies. Tasks to be accomplished must be prioritized, and persons who will accomplish each must be identified. The principal plans for such tasks as student achievement, accreditation, co-curricular activities, master schedule, parent organizations, student trips, and school special events. Managerial competencies are required to get each of these tasks accomplished.

Prior to developing a plan, the principal has to identify what needs to be done and the procedures necessary to accomplish the tasks. Early involvement of participants will facilitate accomplishing tasks. The tasks may involve changing an existing situation or creating a new one to benefit the students. Prior to reaching a decision, the principal must gather as much information as possible from the community and the school. The principal must identify and contact all potential data sources. During the data-gathering process, the principal must analyze information and consider additional sources. This process must be systematic and include the source(s) of the original information, potential data sources, ways to obtain the data, means to analyze the data, who to involve and when, and how to make the decision to create the fairest and best solution(s).

Short-range planning includes the flexibility to reorder long-range plans as unexpected activities occur to enable the school to reach its goals. The principal is also able to see when, and from whom, help is needed to achieve the goals in a timely manner. Effective communication allows the principal to act in proactive ways to accomplish tasks identified in plans.

Schools never have enough resources to meet all the demands placed upon them. Technology is expensive and places tremendous demands on the budget. The proactive principal understands this and makes a plan to maximize available resources. These resources include relocation, renovation, new construction, and allocation of such resources as computer quantity and location, audio-visual equipment quantity and quality, media resources and space, meeting rooms, teacher and staff offices, multipurpose rooms, classrooms, laboratories, cafeterias, playgrounds, physical education indoor and outdoor space, and auxiliary spaces.

Some problems within a school are related to the larger community and require knowledge beyond the school. For example, if drugs allegedly are being sold a few blocks from a school and students supposedly are making purchases during the lunch hour, all information should be obtained and the community should be involved. Community involvement is critical in making a decision on how to handle this problem.

Skill 1.7 **Facilitate the collaborative development of a plan that clearly articulates objectives and strategies for implementing a campus vision.**

When principals commit to become school administrators, they have a passionate notion about how schools should work. This vision often is a collection of thoughts principals have developed during their teaching career or an idea that came from research or reading. The campus vision must be personalized to the campus and should include input from all stakeholders (staff, parents, community) of the individual school, with the principal leading the discussion. A vision is a clear statement of the guarantee given to all students attending a certain school. Embedded in a vision is the idea of the ability to see something that is not readily apparent or that doesn't yet exist. A school's vision should be a picture of the possibilities, reaching into a better future that will benefit the school's children.

How does one gather input about the school's vision? Every conversation with parents and other stakeholders yields information about what is important for their children. The school's history, including its past successes and failures, is an important consideration. The data found in the school's AEIS (Academic Excellence Indicator System) report can steer the stakeholders toward new areas of improvement and focus. Showing a comparison of the school's results to statewide results also will be a conversation starter for areas of celebration or areas to target for improvement. The improvement targets are then delineated in the annual campus improvement plan (CIP) or school improvement plan (SIP) document. The CIP lists the school's goals, along with activities to accomplish the goals, a timeline for completion, and the personnel assigned to monitor goal completion.

Skill 1.8   Align financial, human, and material resources to support implementation of a campus vision.

The principal is the gatekeeper of a school's resources, and resources are more than monetary. Resources include the district budget; student activity funds; Title I and other grant monies; the human resources of parents, staff and volunteers; and the material resources of the school building.

It has been said that everyone in a school is paying attention to what the principal is paying attention to. A principal must make sure that his or her words and actions match and that the vision is the criteria used to identify essentials and priorities. Principals and teachers have limited time and energy. Every task undertaken requires asking, "Will this get me and my staff closer to our vision of what we want to accomplish for children?"

Every financial expenditure requires the signature and approval of the principal. Rather than making the spending decisions based on whim or favoritism, the principal should always be guided by the campus improvement plan and the Campus Performance Objective Council (CPOC). The CPOC is also known as the campus leadership team. As required by Texas Administrative Code, the CPOC will contain members representing the school staff, the parents, and the school community. For example, if funds are requested for an autism conference, but there are no school goals or student needs in this area, then this request should not be funded. However, if the school goals include literacy development, then a request for funding for additional library books may be approved.

The principal also controls the human resources, or the staffing of the school. School staffing models vary from district to district, but all principals have some control of how many teachers and support staff are hired. Principals may make decisions about job descriptions, duties, and assigned responsibilities, as well as appraisal and development of the school staff. It is a waste of human resources to have ineffective staff members continue on the school payroll, so principals should carefully document and remove employees who do not contribute to the school goals. When a need for additional support surfaces, the principal must take an overall look at how staff is being used and reallocate the human resources to meet the need. For example, when teachers are absent and there are not enough substitute teachers to cover the classes, the principal must decide how to manage the classes by combining students or by reassigning office staff or support staff to fill this need.

Resources are always limited, and conflict can occur when stakeholders are denied their requests for spending. Involving the school leadership team in these decisions and keeping the group focused on student achievement will help the principal maintain integrity and will keep the focus on the school vision.

Skill 1.9   **Establish procedures to assess and modify implementation plans to ensure achievement of the campus vision.**

The principal must achieve work through and with others. Clearly defining work and outcomes is important. In this process, the principal establishes procedures to obtain feedback in a timely manner on progress toward the intended outcome(s) of work in progress. Written and oral daily or weekly progress reports monitor the progress of work and provide assistance when needed to meet established deadlines.

The principal should monitor the progress of work through a variety of means. Department chairpersons and grade-level chairpersons are important partners in providing feedback to the principal. When work is assigned across grade and curriculum levels, the chairperson of the tasks should provide timely feedback to the principal. In determining how well progress is being made, the principal can use a variety of resources, such as norm-referenced and criterion-referenced tests, observations, report reviews, checklists, team reviews, and external evaluations to determine how others are performing their work and if they are performing it in a timely manner.

Principals—as instructional leaders—must be present on the campus, regularly visiting classrooms and providing useful feedback to teachers. Principals can provide teachers with techniques and suggestions for improving practice; however, principals must do so while also encouraging and showing support to teachers.

The bottom line is that we cannot, as educational leaders, hold teachers accountable at the end of the year if we do not provide them feedback within the year to let them know how they are doing.

Skill 1.10   **Support innovative thinking and risk taking within the school community and view unsuccessful experiences as learning opportunities.**

> When you start with an honest and diligent effort to determine the truth of the situation, the right decisions often become self-evident . . . You absolutely cannot make a series of good decisions without confronting the brutal facts."
>
> —Jim Collins

Leadership is about creating a climate in which the truth is heard and the brutal facts confronted. We often choose to ignore brutal facts because they might make people uncomfortable, or be inconvenient, should we acknowledge them. Education has a strong moral component—it should enable people to work together to achieve higher purposes that serve both the individual and the collective good. We can only move forward by learning from one another's successes and failures. Change cannot be achieved if teachers identify with only their own classrooms—they must be concerned with the success of other teachers at the school. Looking at data disaggregated by teachers, student groups, and item analysis enables the school staff to confront areas of needed improvement, share best practices, and plan for the desired results. When teachers disaggregate school-wide test data, they should look for the test questions that most lowered their school's scores. What skills are associated with those questions? Those are the skills on which to focus in the year ahead.

This cycle of data analysis, action planning, assessment for results will lead to continuous improvement. Failure cannot be an option, and principals, as courageous leaders, must continually remind the school community that any setbacks are temporary. Knowing what did not work helps the school find solutions that will raise student achievement.

Skill 1.11 Acknowledge and celebrate the contributions of students, staff, parents, and community members toward realization of the campus vision.

Because communication is a process in which a person or group learns another's ideas, attitudes, and beliefs, communication is central to supervisory behavior. For a positive interaction to occur, the educational leader must understand the cause-and-effect relationship between his or her actions and the reactions of others.

Positive Behaviors

Show an interest in the work of others.
- Cause: Assistant principals and principals should note student and teacher performance and offer assistance as indicated. Principals should learn about teachers' and students' work by first-hand observation.
- Effect: Workers at all levels will recognize the consideration given to their achievements and will feel more comfortable seeking help to solve problems.

Be knowledgeable of job requirements for all personnel and give praise.
- Cause: Supervisors must evaluate performance on job descriptors. Focus on good performance; avoid being overly critical. Pass on compliments to higher-level management.
- Effect: Employees respond with better performance when supervisors can note specific facets of the employees' work.

Exhibit pleasing personality traits.
- Cause: Being courteous, fair, and honest and having high integrity are desirable because supervisors serve as role models for the type of behavior expected of everyone in the system.
- Effect: Workers in the system will strive to emulate desirable personality traits. Members of the community form an opinion of the system based on the personalities of educational leaders whom they meet at school functions or through other community organizations.

Stand by convictions.
- Cause: Supervisors should formulate strong beliefs, state them unequivocally, and support them despite opposition.
- Effect: Students, teachers, and other leaders do not respect fence-sitters. They may not always agree with the stated beliefs, but they will defend the right to express them.

Show confidence in employees' abilities and allow self-direction.
- Cause: Supervisors at all levels must recognize the professional qualities of other professionals. Allow subordinates to work flexibly within prescribed guidelines.
- Effect: Employees will become confident decision makers, capable of completing their jobs without constant supervision.

Be firm in following school and district guidelines for student discipline.
- Cause: School administrators should consistently adhere to discipline policy. Show no favoritism and be fair. Principals should receive support from the superintendent and the school board.
- Effect: Students will know that their misdeeds will be dealt with efficiently. Teachers will be able to manage classrooms more effectively.

Exhibit a sense of humor.
- Cause: A sincere sense of humor—not sarcasm or facetiousness—encourages an amiable environment for communication. It can be used to release tension and to foster the relaxed climate in which comfortable exchange can occur.
- Effect: Employees recognize a supervisor's ability to establish rapport by not taking herself or the demands of her position too seriously. An occasional shared laugh at some absurdity puts the situation in perspective and creates a climate in which all parties can view the issue constructively.

The principal competency of *organizational sensitivity* relates to the principal's awareness of the effect of his or her behavior and decisions on others. The objectives for evaluation include the following:

- Using tactful oral and written responses to persons within and outside the school
- Informing members of the school community of information that is or could be relevant to them
- Considering the position, emotions, and attitudes of others when organizing, planning, and making decisions

COMPETENCY 2.0   **THE PRINCIPAL KNOWS HOW TO COMMUNICATE AND COLLABORATE WITH ALL MEMBERS OF THE SCHOOL COMMUNITY, RESPOND TO DIVERSE INTERESTS AND NEEDS, AND MOBILIZE RESOURCES TO PROMOTE STUDENT SUCCESS.**

Skill 2.1   **Communicate effectively with families and other community members in varied educational contexts.**

In any organization or business, more than half of the administrator or supervisor's time is spent communicating with others. Good communication is essential to any educational organization; the more effective the communication process, the more successful the education process. The roles of the administrator as goal setter, task organizer, employee motivator, decision maker, and public relations agent are facilitated by the ability to manage the communication process effectively.

Communication is the exchange of information (message) between a sender and a receiver. The process involves six steps:

1. Ideating: Developing the idea or message to be communicated
2. Encoding: Organizing the idea into a sequence of symbols (written or spoken words, nonverbal cues, or medium) to convey the message
3. Transmitting: Delivering the encoded message through a medium (face to face, telephone, written statements, video or computer products)
4. Receiving: Claiming of the message by the receiver, who must be a good reader/listener, attentive to the message's meaning
5. Decoding: The receiver's translation of the message
6. Acting: Action taken by the receiver in response to the message (ignore, store, react)

Feedback to the sender that the message has been received and understood is what makes communication reciprocal.

Educational leadership training programs often explain the communication process in terms of sources and channels. The main source elements are expertise, credibility, composure, and dynamism. The ability to incorporate these elements into idea presentation results in the most persuasive communication.

The means of message transmission are referred to as channels. Some characteristics of channels are the need to use different media for different audiences, the need to use recognizable and respected channels, the need to select mass media that serve different purposes, and the recognition of personal channels as more effective than mass media in changing opinions.

Direction of Communication (Formal)

1. Downward: The transmission of information from people at higher levels to people at lower levels (superintendents to principals, principals to faculty and staff)
2. Upward: The transmission of information (usually feedback) from people who are at lower levels to people who are at higher levels (principals to directors of instruction, department heads/team leaders to principals)
3. Lateral (horizontal): Transmission of information between people on the same level in the organizational structure (assistant superintendent of instruction to assistant superintendent of facilities)
4. Diagonal: Direct transmission of information between people at different levels in the hierarchy (usually reserved for instances in which information cannot go through proper channels in a timely fashion—for example, special reports from principals that go directly to the superintendent or assistant superintendents for transmission to the state)

There is a fifth form of communication, apart from direction or formal practice—the grapevine. In reality, the majority of information transmitted by employees laterally is carried through the grapevine. Its face-to-face informality transmits information rapidly.

Administrators should be aware of the operation of the school grapevine and incorporate its positive aspects into the communication structure. The negative aspect of unsubstantiated rumor-passing will be overridden if the administrator takes the following actions:
- Keeps employees informed about matters relevant to the school or district and about issues that impact the employees' jobs
- Provides employees the opportunity to express attitudes and feelings about issues
- Tests employees' reactions to information before making decisions
- Builds morale by repeating positive reactions/comments made by employees to higher-level administrators or the community, and vice versa

Teaching professionals do not like feeling that they are being kept in the dark or are getting only partial or untimely information. Telling teachers in a faculty meeting that the district is going to reduce the faculty at their school before transfer provisions have been established will create distrust. It may seem an open gesture on the principal's part, but the timing is wrong.

Barriers to Communication
- The communication process requires that the sender and receiver have a common frame of reference. Because we all interpret information based on previous experience and cultural background, receivers may interpret the ideas in messages differently than the sender intended. For example, information delivered during contract negotiations is interpreted differently

by union representatives than by district contract negotiators. These distorted perceptions arise because the participants are operating from different frames of reference. To make the communication effective, all parties must realize that the goal of the talks is to spend funds in the most educationally sound manner.

- Filtering is a barrier that occurs during transmission of information from one level to another. It may be intentional or unintentional. In downward communication, it may be the omission of some of the message or improper encoding for the intended audience. Administrators frequently deliver information on a need-to-know basis or deliver only positive information, fearing that negative information will damage the decoding process. This confuses the receivers about the message's intent or makes them feel patronized. In upward communication, employees may limit information to those facts that shed favorable light on their personal performance because of previous experience with inconsistent or arbitrary evaluations.

- Another barrier results from improper listening skills. The receiver must heed the entire message, decode it nonjudgmentally, and seek clarification of any unclear points. This happens best when the sender creates a nonthreatening environment in which the listener can practice nonevaluative listening.

- Biases against race, gender, or status can prejudice receivers against a message. Senders can suggest bias by words, nonverbal clues, and attitudes. A male principal with chauvinist attitudes may alienate female teachers; a male teacher who resents a female principal may tune her out.

Overcoming these barriers is an administrative responsibility. To establish effective communication, the principal should do the following:
- Establish trust by sincerely correlating message and behavior. Never being available after emphasizing an open-door policy will undermine trust.
- Listen carefully and provide open channels for feedback. Avoid giving nonverbal cues that contradict the message.
- Understand and respect employees' needs, interests, and attitudes. Allow discussion, even disagreement. The important thing is that employees know they are being heard.
- Time information delivery properly. Timing affects the manner in which employees perceive the message. Avoid leaking partial information. Transmit accurate information in time for employees to provide feedback.
- Use appropriate media for transmitting the message. Written or face-to-face communication is necessary when the message concerns a single receiver or when the message concerns a group with common interests. Oral or video presentations are appropriate for delivering information that

affects a department or faculty, such as safety measures or reporting abuse.

The educational leader must be adept in the many skills of communication.

Skill 2.2   Apply skills for building consensus and managing conflict.

Effective communication and conflict resolution relies on the principal's ability to project a positive self-image and to instill in others the feelings that foster self-esteem.

1. Seek understanding, not judgment. Do not argue points of disagreement. Try to understand what the sender is saying. Identify specific points of agreement and disagreement. Paraphrase areas of agreement to determine if interpretation is correct. Point out areas of disagreement for further examination and discussion.
2. Practice active listening skills. Recognize that receiver decoding skills are affected by feelings and perception about the sender that hinder receipt of the message. As receivers ask questions or paraphrase your message, focus on their ideas, ask specific questions to reveal their level of attentiveness, and avoid drawing heated emotional responses. Avoid defensive or attacking responses. Remember that open communication is based on reciprocal trust.

The principal competency of *self-presentation* is the ability to convey a message effectively and to share ideas in a nonevaluative manner.

The principal should:
- communicate ideas (his or her own and others') in a clear, informative way in both one-on-one and group situations;
- stimulate others to ask questions about their own issues; and
- present himself or herself in a way that is not viewed as controlling or demanding conformity.

Consensus Decision Making

Consensus decision making is a group decision-making process that seeks the consent of all participants. *Consensus* may be defined professionally as an acceptable resolution, one that all participants can support even if it is not their first choice.

Consensus decision making is an alternative to commonly practiced adversarial decision-making processes. Robert's Rules of Order, for instance, is a process many organizations use. The goal of Robert's Rules is to structure the debate and passage of proposals that win approval through majority vote. This process does not emphasize the goal of full agreement. Critics of Robert's Rules believe that the process can involve adversarial debate and the formation of competing factions. These dynamics may harm group member relationships and undermine the ability of a group to cooperatively implement a contentious decision.

Consensus decision making attempts to address the problems of both Robert's Rules of Order and top-down models. Proponents claim that outcomes of the consensus process include the following:

- Better decisions: By including the input of all stakeholders, the resulting proposals may better address all potential concerns.
- Better implementation: A process that includes and respects all parties and generates as much agreement as possible sets the stage for greater cooperation in implementing the resulting decisions.
- Better group relationships: A cooperative, collaborative group atmosphere can foster greater group cohesion and interpersonal connection.

Agreement vs. consent

Giving consent does not necessarily mean that the proposal being considered is one's first choice. Group members can vote their consent to a proposal to cooperate with the direction of the group rather than insist on their personal preference. Sometimes the vote on a proposal is framed, "Is this proposal something you can live with?" This relaxed threshold for a yes vote can achieve full consent. This full consent, however, does not mean that everyone is in full agreement. Consent must be genuine and cannot be obtained by force, duress, or fraud.

Benefits of consensus decision making

- Inclusive participation engages and empowers the group.
- It requires a commitment to work together and increases cooperation.
- It creates shared understanding through discussion that bridges differences.
- It equalizes the distribution of power in a group.
- It can create better decisions that are more representative of the larger community.
- It creates more ownership and commitment.
- It results in more effective implementation because the entire group takes action on the project or plan.

Choose consensus building in the following situations:

- There are many stakeholders and perspectives for a complex problem.
- People are willing to participate.
- The group has authority to make decisions and will be affected by them.
- Creative solutions are needed.
- You need everyone involved to be committed to the decision or plan.

Choose alternative methods of decision making in the following situations:

- There is no common goal or purpose.
- There is an unwillingness to participate or cooperate.
- The group has low trust or a lack of commitment.
- Time is limited or there is an emergency.
- Needed information is not available.
- People are polarized on issues or values.
- The problem has a clear solution.

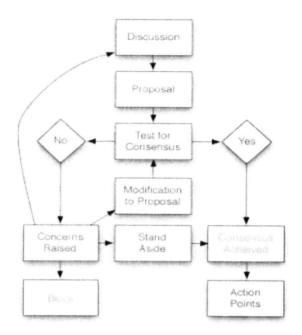

Skill 2.3 Implement effective strategies for systematically communicating with and gathering input from all campus stakeholders.

Principals should seek input from parents in systematic and planned ways. Annual surveys, parent informational nights, and parent advisory committees allow principals to receive valuable input on a variety of topics. Principals benefit from opportunities to learn the community's perception of the school and what issues might impact the school's progress. Public relations must be carefully organized. People who deliver Information must have accurate information, understand their roles as disseminators of the information, and provide appropriate channels for feedback. Members of the public must perceive that they are being given complete, timely information by officials who respect their feelings and sincerely want feedback. Many principals use a key communicator email list to disperse information immediately. Each parent who receives the information will not have to rely on rumors or gossip from the neighborhood. This ability to communicate quickly and effectively with key members of the community is especially important when a crisis situation develops at a school. Having a key communicator email list keeps parents informed and prevents them from hearing about an issue from a biased media presentation.

Skill 2.4   Develop and implement strategies for effective internal and external communications.

Principals must have effective internal communication systems in place for the school to meet its goals. Printed weekly or daily agendas keep the school staff informed about activities, meetings, and events. There also should be opportunities for dialogue so that school staff members can talk to one another about questions, problems, or concerns.

In situations that might have media coverage, the principal should inform the school staff before they hear about the situation on the news. Especially when the news is big, principals and school districts should prepare employees with talking points and give them a chance to ask questions and ensure they understand what's happening so they can adequately answer questions. The staff always should be aware of the district's policies regarding communication with media outlets.

Transmission Methods

- Written (for internal audiences)
  - Daily announcements for students and faculty
  - Student newspapers
  - Superintendent's monthly newsletter to faculties
  - Reports of school board meetings
  - Memorandums from all levels, downward or laterally

- Written (for external audiences)
  - Principal's newsletter to parents
  - Annual reports
  - News releases

- Oral (for internal audiences)
  - Daily announcements or other student broadcasts over intercom or closed-circuit television
  - Meetings of committees of students, parents, teachers, and administrators
  - Faculty meetings
  - Student government or club meetings
  - Pep rallies

- Oral (for external audiences)
  - o Recorded promotions of schools or school-related events
  - o Direct telephone contacts with parents
  - o Student presentations—concerts, plays, content area fairs, awards ceremonies
  - o Radio and television programs to promote school events or discuss education issues

See also Skill 2.1, Skill 2.3, and Skill 2.5.

Skill 2.5   Develop and implement a comprehensive program of community relations that effectively involves and informs multiple constituencies, including the media.

For proper operations, schools require good communication. Parents need to communicate information to teachers and other school staff members; students need to communicate to teachers and administrators; administrators need to communicate to parents, community members, students, and district leaders; and teachers need to communicate to students, parents, and administrators. With so many groups and so few methods of direct communication (after all, how often can a teacher leave his or her classroom to make phone calls?), it is imperative that principals find and provide stakeholders access to a variety of communication tools. Additionally, principals must utilize a wide variety of communication techniques to effectively convey their messages.

For example, although email is a great communication tool, it ceases to be effective if responses are not given in a timely manner or if responses are short or terse, lacking in emotional character. There are a variety of techniques that can be used in person-to-person communication, small meetings, large-group information sessions, electronic communication, and informal communication:

- *Active listening.* Even when the ultimate goal for communication is to send a message from the speaker to the audience, the speaker must demonstrate that he or she is attentive to audience needs and reacts to concerns and questions. Speakers can be active listeners by rephrasing questions, summarizing stated ideas, and purposely integrating audience concerns into the message.
- *Personal.* There are few things more boring than listening to someone give a prepared speech, with no emotion and little personality or humor. Even with a serious topic, principals can impart a sense of humanity into any speech or communicative act. It helps people feel comfortable and open.
- *Focusing on nonverbal cues.* Facial expressions, posture, gestures, and eye contact all make a huge difference in communicating ideas effectively. It is especially important that principals continuously look interested, informed, and proactive as they present information to people.

- *Balanced.* Principals who carefully consider the needs of all groups are most effective. Principals, therefore, should seek to treat each group fairly and speak about each group with respect.

Overall, communication strategies help convey messages in formal and informal situations. New principals can pay close attention to these strategies; eventually they will become internalized and feel natural.

Practices of Good Communication

- Think first. This applies both to preparation before a formal written or oral presentation and to pausing to gather your thoughts before impromptu speaking.
- Stay informed. Never speak or write without preparation or attempt to discuss matters beyond your scope of knowledge. Stay abreast of education issues, especially in leadership and supervision. Read journals and participate in professional organizations. Keep a notebook of newsletters, clippings, and resource lists that you can highlight and use to add credibility to your communication.
- Assess your audience. Know the addressed person or group's interests and attitudes. Show respect for their points of view by your tone and pace as well as your volume and posture when speaking. Demonstrate a genuine liking for people by a willingness to share your ideas and solicit their responses.
- Focus attention on your message, not on yourself. A little nervousness about communicating well is normal even for practiced writers/speakers. Familiarity with your topic; the ability to develop clear, complete sentences; and the use of concrete examples will enhance delivery.
- Speak/write correctly. Use of proper grammar, usage, and sentence structure will allow listeners/readers to concentrate on what you say, rather than on distracting language errors.
- Be concise. Get to the point and then quit. Use words and sentences economically. Being unnecessarily long-winded is a sure way to lose your audience.
- Use delivery techniques to your advantage. In written communication, be sure to state the main idea, give examples or explanations, and link the ideas in a logical manner. In oral communication, use eye contact to demonstrate sincerity and hold listener attention. Use body language to add enthusiasm and conviction to your words, but avoid expansive or repetitive movements that can distract. Modulate the pitch and volume of your voice for emphasis.
- Listen thoughtfully to feedback. In face-to-face communication, be aware of nonverbal cues that suggest either active listening or boredom.

Skill 2.6   Provide varied and meaningful opportunities for parents/caregivers to be engaged in the education of their children.

Research has proven that when schools and parents work together, children receive higher grades and test scores. A key responsibility of the principal is to continually provide opportunities for parents/caregivers to be involved in the education of their children.

Training the school staff on how to communicate with parents is the place to begin. Teachers must understand that parents want to hear positive information about their child, not just reports about negative behavior or academic failure. Teachers should also be discouraged from using educational jargon that parents may not understand. Principals should check the reception area of the school to see how parents are treated when they arrive at the school. If everyone at the school shows appreciation for parents who are trying to be involved, then parent involvement will increase.

Finding and removing barriers to parent involvement is important to a school's success. Here are some ideas that will increase opportunities for parent involvement in a school:

1. Offer incentives for parents to attend meetings. Giving away food, books, and other door prizes helps increase attendance.
2. Have students perform at school meetings. All parents like to see their children on stage and will attend meetings for that reason.
3. Call parents and personally invite them to a meeting.
4. Provide rides to meetings for parents lacking transportation.
5. Open a Parent Center. Stock it with parenting books and other resources so that parents will have a place to increase their own knowledge and to network with other parents.
6. Hold parent workshops. Topics such as working with your ADHD child, computer literacy, and how to read with your child will increase student success and parent involvement.
7. Ask teachers to provide several opportunities each year for parents to come to school and look at a portfolio of their child's work. The teacher can circulate and answer questions. Parent and child can also work on skills or projects together with the teacher present to assist, explain, or clarify the expectations.

Skill 2.7   Establish partnerships with parents/caregivers, businesses, and others in the community to strengthen programs and support campus goals.

Public information management is a systematic communication process between an educational organization and its public, both within and outside the schools. It is the exchange of information designed to encourage public interest in and understanding of education. A principal shows concern for the school's image through impressions created by students and staff and manages both these impressions and public information about the school by (1) advertising successes and (2) controlling the flow of negative information.

To be effective, communication between school leaders and the public must be open, honest, and unbiased. The attitudes of parents and members of the community have been adversely affected by reports of the decline in American education and media coverage that appears to focus on negative perceptions. Despite the general perception of poor public education, the majority of parents surveyed nationally expressed satisfaction with their children's schools and teachers. The most positive feedback resulted when parents felt that their concerns were being heard and addressed and that they were involved in the decision-making process.

Public relations must be carefully organized and good communications practices followed at all times.

Public Relations Process

1. Public information management requires analyzing the community attitude toward educational issues. The required school improvement surveys conducted each spring in many schools provide not only feedback on the issues but also priorities for addressing them. Public workshops and meetings allow community members to become involved in learning about budget, discipline, and academic issues. Information gathering should be structured to obtain the most scientific results, that is, ensuring a representative sampling by mailing surveys rather than entrusting their delivery and return to students.

2. The planning phase requires setting specific goals and designing the campaign to achieve the goals. During this phase, educational leaders should determine the audiences, forums, and time frames in which their message(s) will be delivered to the public. A presentation to senior citizens concerning a tax increase may require a different slant than a presentation to people who have children in the schools. Issues that require voter decisions should be presented with ample time for study and cooperative decision making, or at least discussion.

3. Following the communication process is equally important whether information is delivered internally or externally. Student groups are a segment of the internal public and should be treated with the same open respect as elements of the community at large. Each information campaign must be encoded with specific audiences in mind. Selecting the appropriate media (transmission methods) to convey the message greatly affects the outcome. First-approach media are usually newsletters to parents, press releases, annual reports—any written document that can

be distributed to the intended audiences. Follow-up transmissions include open houses, school committee or school board meetings, education fairs—any face-to-face communication that brings the public and school representatives together for a two-way exchange.

4. Finally, school/district officials must evaluate the results of the public relations effort. Some evaluation is immediate, as in the election of a candidate or the passage of a bond issue. Periodic evaluations in the form of brief questionnaires in school newsletters, telephone surveys, or written assessments at the end of public meetings can help test the public's understanding and the level of community support.

Other Considerations

1. Schools must establish good relationships with the media. When there are more complaints in the Letters to the Editor section of the newspaper than there are news articles about school events, there is obviously a poor interaction between media and the schools. Of course, there are several reasons for the amount of educational coverage provided by various media:

   - Small local newspapers give broader coverage to local issues/events. They may devote a whole page or section to school/classroom events.
   - Newspapers have to evaluate the "newsworthiness" of stories. For example, local spelling bees get better coverage than Mrs. Clarke's debate class's mock trial because one spelling bee winner in each district will compete nationally. Most newspapers consider a story about vandalism at a school or a union walkout more newsworthy than a piece about students working at an animal shelter. Large city newspapers and television stations focus more on national and state news and regrettably often focus on educational issues that have negative or sensational impact.
   - Local radio and television stations may be a better venue for school news than newspapers. They may broadcast interviews with school officials, teachers, or students or debates on education issues that have local impact.

2. School/district publications—newsletters, information brochures, handbooks, annual reports—may be useful in providing a positive link with the community.

3. Displays of student work in public places—malls, building lobbies, and business waiting rooms—provide visual evidence of student achievement.

Skill 2.8 Communicate and work effectively with diverse groups in the school community to ensure that all students have an equal opportunity for educational success.

According to Dr. James Comer, professor of child psychiatry at Yale University, "No significant learning takes place without a significant relationship." Principals should be aware of this insight as they seek to create productive relationships in the school community regardless of the socioeconomic, ethnic, or educational background of the stakeholders. Community groups, such as churches, businesses, and daycares that are engaged in the education process, are invaluable partners, increasing the likelihood that children will be successful in meeting the learning goals of the school.

A principal should seek out diversity on school committees so that all stakeholder groups are giving feedback about the school. When recruiting volunteers, principals should reach out to underrepresented groups. This can be done with personal phone calls, a willingness to meet at unusual times and places to accommodate work schedules, or simply asking for input, even if it has to be by phone. Realizing that some people in your school community have had negative personal school-related experiences can make you more sensitive to the barriers to involvement. Principals must also realize that community members and parents are often impacted by mental and physical fatigue stemming from economic stress. To assume that the lack of involvement means a lack of caring pushes people away instead of drawing them into your school.

Here are some things that can begin to build strong relationships with diverse groups in your school community:

Take steps to ensure that your staff knows your clientele. Tour the community with your staff so they see where the students live and what resources may be available in the community.

Treat all visitors to your building with a high level of professionalism. Be willing to accommodate their preferences concerning day and time for meeting, then arrive on time and be well prepared. Schools lose credibility with parents and the community when they appear unaware about what is happening with a child or are unsure of what to do about it. When confronted with a problem, do not be afraid to admit mistakes. Always apologize for any mistakes.

Administrators must ensure that all communication with the community is clear and effective. Lack of communication and miscommunication account for nearly 80% of problems or conflicts. You can develop key communicator email lists to get word out quickly if there is a school problem, event, or need that involves the community. Utilize neighborhood newsletters and local newspapers to get out the facts about the school. Don't assume that everyone knows what you are trying to accomplish with your students. Make sure that language barriers are not an issue. Be aware of written or verbal language that is overloaded with educational verbiage.

Make the effort to find out what the community groups are thinking and feeling. You can do this by regularly using short surveys that address very specific topics. Make a few phone calls or visits each week to ask how community groups think things are going at the school. Be sure to include a diverse population on your site council or school improvement team.

Find out what the school can do to support community efforts. Local restaurants may need seasonal decorations that your art classes can provide. A nursing home in the area may enjoy a holiday concert from your school choir. Local churches may need help with a variety of service projects. Older students may be able to assist with babysitting at community functions. When your school contributes to the needs of the community, you will find the community groups more willing to involve themselves in the success of the school.

Ask the school staff to be visible in the community. When the school staff frequents restaurants or churches, ask them to identify themselves to the people in charge. Knowing that some of the customer base comes from the local school will increase the community group's interest and participation in school events and programs.

Don't be afraid to ask for help. When you've invested time in building relationships with community groups, when you've actively sought their input, then you can ask for help without hesitation. Employees of local businesses may be able to come at lunch and tutor at-risk children. Donations may be given that will provide students with school supplies or other needed items. Healthcare services may be provided at low cost to families in need. Always remember to follow up with a letter of thanks for the support you receive. Involving the students in the displays of gratitude adds the personal connection that will keep the community involved in the school.

Skill 2.9   Respond to pertinent political, social, and economic issues in the internal and external environment.

Schools do not exist in a vacuum. They are open systems, which means that they are interrelated with the environments within which they exist. The external environment of schools includes parents, businesses, taxpayers, and politicians. All of these are important to schools because in some way their actions affect the operations of a school. Legislatures, colleges, and other governmental or educational agencies increasingly influence schools. However, schools cannot be everything to all constituents. All organizations depend upon the environment of which they are a part for resources and other types of support. Hence, schools must maintain public relations campaigns regarding their effectiveness. In addition, it is important for school leaders to know who has and exercises power in a community.

Community aspirations and values have a significant role in the operations of a school. Schools, to an extent, serve the needs of the community in which they are located. Schools must relate and react to the changing environmental conditions as they relate to the demographics of the community and the economic base. Knowing the types of jobs in the community enables the educational organization to provide education for students relevant to the demands of the local economy. If the school significantly departs from the standards and norms of the community, a school leader can experience difficulty.

Recently, the federal government has played a greater part in school operations. Generally, while schools once were influenced primarily by local customs and needs, they are now increasingly the subject of federally mandated accountability systems. No Child Left Behind (NCLB), while leaving specific operational policies to local regulation, has put governmental and public oversight into the mix, and schools increasingly must demonstrate that all students meet achievement standards. Therefore, schools recently have been shaped by public perception, governmental regulation, and the fear of declining enrollment or state takeover. In many ways, this federal law has encouraged schools to become more competitive with one another for students, attention, and funding.

Mandatory retention is part of the NCLB standards in Texas. Grade retention has long been viewed as a logical, straightforward strategy for students who are achieving below their grade level or experiencing chronic behavior problems. Increasingly, it also is viewed as a preferable alternative to social promotion. Some educators and administrators believe that giving struggling students another year to mature academically, behaviorally, or socially will help them. Other school leaders believe that grade retention is necessary to meet their school's annual yearly progress (AYP) and other performance mandates. In Texas, retention in grade 5 is mandatory for students who cannot pass the state tests in reading and in math.

Research reveals that neither grade retention nor social promotion alone is an effective strategy for improving students' academic, behavioral, and social and emotional success. Like so much in education, what is most effective is a targeted approach that addresses students' academic, social, and mental health issues and links specific evidence-based interventions to a student's individual needs (Algozzine, Ysseldyke, and Elliot, 2002; Shinn and Walker, 2012).

Confidence in public education has eroded over the past several decades. Numerous private, parochial, charter, and other types of schools have emerged during this period. Concomitant with these shifts is an increased attention to providing vouchers for parents to use in selecting a school for their children. The public perceptions of students, faculty, staff, administration, and the total school are significant in the community's attitude about a school. Management of a school requires a clear understanding of the importance of this public perception as well as techniques to handle successes and problems.

COMPETENCY 3.0 **THE PRINCIPAL KNOWS HOW TO ACT WITH INTEGRITY, FAIRNESS, AND IN AN ETHICAL AND LEGAL MANNER.**

Skill 3.1 **Model and promote the highest standard of conduct, ethical principles, and integrity in decision making, actions, and behaviors.**

Principals are leaders. Their behavior, stated communication, and implied communication have a tremendous impact on those with whom they work. Others often follow the lead of the principal. If a principal is calm in difficult situations, the students, parents, staff, and faculty will usually assume this position; the reverse is also true.

A principal who resolves conflict in a systematic, fair manner promotes this kind of behavior within the school. Others in the school community closely observe and follow the means a principal uses to share information and reach decisions.

The principal who shows partiality or insists that his or her position is the only one will not obtain meaningful input from those with whom he or she is working. In this type of environment, people will say what they expect the principal to say, say nothing, or agree with the principal's views. In this case, the best results are not achieved since the best collective thinking of the learning community is not a part of the planning, implementation, and evaluation of the work of the school. If the principal appears to close or open up discussion, others in the environment will respond accordingly. A strong principal realizes that there are times when decisions must be made and makes them in a timely fashion. For example, if a person enters the campus with a gun, the principal must take action to keep everyone safe. If teachers have a conflict, the principal must resolve the problem before it becomes a major deterrent to achievement of organizational goals.

Integrity

Having integrity means living in accordance to your deepest values: you're honest with everyone, and you always keep your word. How do you do this as a principal?

Step 1: Define your values

You can't live by values if you don't know what you truly believe in. So, start by defining your core values. These are the values that, no matter what the consequence, you're not going to compromise on.

Step 2: Analyze every choice you make

Often, people cut corners or make bad choices when they think no one is watching. Having integrity means that, no matter what, you make the right choice—especially when no one is watching!

You'll usually know what's right and wrong, although sometimes you might need some quiet time to figure it out. If you're not sure what the right choice is, ask yourself these two questions:

1. If my choice was printed on the front page of the newspaper for everyone to see, would I feel okay about it?

2. If I make this choice, will I feel okay with myself afterward?

Remember, honesty and integrity aren't values that you should live by when it's convenient; they're values that you should live by all the time. This includes the big choices and the little choices—the choices everyone sees and the choices that no one sees.

Step 3: Encourage integrity

People with integrity often share certain characteristics: they're humble, they have a strong sense of self, they have high self-esteem, and they're self-confident. These characteristics are important, because sometimes you'll be under intense pressure from others to make the wrong choice.

Work on building and improving these characteristics within yourself, so that you have the strength and courage to do the right thing when the time comes. Build your self-confidence and self-esteem and work on developing character. Spend time getting to know yourself and what you believe in. Develop friendships and work relationships with others who demonstrate integrity and who will support your decisions.

Further tips

- Learn how to be assertive, so that you can defend an ethical position from an adult point of view, without whining or being aggressive.

- Avoid white lies. They may seem harmless, but tiny lies are still lies. Always tell the truth.

- Learn to take responsibility for your actions. If you make a mistake, own up to it immediately and do whatever it takes to correct the situation.

- Keep your word and don't make promises that you know you can't keep.

- Keep in mind that in times of fear, disaster, and chaos, the temptation is even greater to make a wrong choice. Use these opportunities to demonstrate your true character.

- Avoid seeming self-satisfied or priggish when you're acting with integrity. Stay humble and down to earth, don't look for approval, and, when you can, try to let people save face.

Skill 3.2   Implement policies and procedures that promote professional educator compliance with the Code of Ethics and Standard Practices for Texas Educators.

The state of Texas has assembled a variety of statements to guide the professional conduct of school employees. The basic concept is that because public school educators work with children all day, they must conduct themselves in an appropriate manner. Furthermore, when certain concerns about students arise, educators are mandated by the state to submit reports. For example, indications of child abuse or indications that the student has attempted suicide would require that a teacher follow specified reporting procedures. Principals must remind teachers of this regularly.

The Code of Ethics and Standard Practices for Texas Educators was rewritten in 2002 by the State Board for Educator Certification (SBEC), the entity responsible for enforcing the Code of Ethics. According to SBEC, revision was necessary because ambiguity in the old code made it difficult to enforce.

The new code provides a more specific statement of expected conduct for Texas educators. The code has been streamlined and clarified and now contains a statement of purpose and a list of enforceable standards. The statement of purpose outlines general ethical guidelines for educators; however, the statement of purpose is not enforceable. The list of enforceable principles has been reduced from five to three, but the remaining principles are clearer and more easily understood and enforced. The first two principles in the old code (Principle I – Professional ethical conduct and Principle II – Professional practices and performance) have been merged into one broader principle entitled Professional Ethical Conduct, Practices and Performance. Additionally, the former Principle V (Ethical conduct toward parents and community) has been removed. This was done because the items in Principle V did not properly and clearly identify the standards of conduct required of educators in an enforceable manner. The goals in the former Principle V have been incorporated into the statement of purpose.

**Revised Code of Ethics and Standard
Practices for Texas Educators**
(Effective Sept. 1, 2002)

The Texas educator shall comply with standard practices and ethical conduct toward students, professional colleagues, school officials, parents, and members of the community and shall safeguard academic freedom. The Texas educator, in maintaining the dignity of the profession, shall respect and obey the law, demonstrate personal integrity, and exemplify honesty. The Texas educator, in exemplifying ethical relations with colleagues, shall extend just and equitable treatment to all members of the profession. The Texas educator, in accepting a position of public trust, shall measure success by the progress of each student toward realization of his or her potential as an effective citizen. The Texas educator, in fulfilling responsibilities in the community, shall cooperate with parents and others to improve the public schools of the community.

Enforceable Standards

I. Professional Ethical Conduct, Practices and Performance.

Standard 1.1. The educator shall not knowingly engage in deceptive practices regarding official policies of the school district or educational institution.

Standard 1.2. The educator shall not knowingly misappropriate, divert or use monies, personnel, property or equipment committed to his or her charge for personal gain or advantage.

Standard 1.3. The educator shall not submit fraudulent requests for reimbursement, expenses or pay.

Standard 1.4. The educator shall not use institutional or professional privileges for personal or partisan advantage.

Standard 1.5. The educator shall neither accept nor offer gratuities, gifts, or favors that impair professional judgment or to obtain special advantage. This standard shall not restrict the acceptance of gifts or tokens offered and accepted openly from students, parents or other persons or organizations in recognition or appreciation of service.

Standard 1.6. The educator shall not falsify records, or direct or coerce others to do so.

Standard 1.7. The educator shall comply with state regulations, written local school board policies and other applicable state and federal laws.

Standard 1.8. The educator shall apply for, accept, offer, or assign a position or a responsibility on the basis of professional qualifications.

II. Ethical Conduct Toward Professional Colleagues.

Standard 2.1. The educator shall not reveal confidential health or personnel information concerning colleagues unless disclosure serves lawful professional purposes or is required by law.

Standard 2.2. The educator shall not harm others by knowingly making false statements about a colleague or the school system.

Standard 2.3. The educator shall adhere to written local school board policies and state and federal laws regarding the hiring, evaluation, and dismissal of personnel.

Standard 2.4. The educator shall not interfere with a colleague's exercise of political, professional or citizenship rights and responsibilities.

Standard 2.5. The educator shall not discriminate against or coerce a colleague on the basis of race, color, religion, national origin, age, sex, disability, or family status.

Standard 2.6. The educator shall not use coercive means or promise of special treatment in order to influence professional decisions or colleagues.

Standard 2.7. The educator shall not retaliate against any individual who has filed a complaint with the SBEC under this chapter.

III. Ethical Conduct Toward Students.

Standard 3.1. The educator shall not reveal confidential information concerning students unless disclosure serves lawful professional purposes or is required by law.

Standard 3.2. The educator shall not knowingly treat a student in a manner that adversely affects the student's learning, physical health, mental health or safety.

Standard 3.3. The educator shall not deliberately or knowingly misrepresent facts regarding a student.

Standard 3.4. The educator shall not exclude a student from participation in a program, deny benefits to a student, or grant an advantage to a student on the basis of race, color, sex, disability, national origin, religion, or family status.

Standard 3.5. The educator shall not engage in physical mistreatment of a student.

Standard 3.6. The educator shall not solicit or engage in sexual conduct or a romantic relationship with a student.

Standard 3.7. The educator shall not furnish alcohol or illegal/unauthorized drugs to any student or knowingly allow any student to consume alcohol or illegal/unauthorized drugs in the presence of the educator.

Skill 3.3   Apply knowledge of ethical issues affecting education.

The field of education is increasingly controversial. School principals are faced with numerous ethical issues at both the classroom and building levels. Keeping this in mind, principals must continuously reflect upon the decisions they make and the examples they set for their students, parents, and colleagues. An effective school principal will work to develop skills and strategies to handle these ethical challenges. There are various ethical frameworks and perspectives on ethics to help principals face these issues. The following are some of the critical ethical issues currently affecting education:

- High-stakes testing
- Special education
- Retention vs. social promotion
- Zero-tolerance policies
- Teacher evaluation/merit pay
- Separation of church and state
- Creationism vs. evolution
- Teaching contracts and teacher tenure
- The right to due process

Principals must handle ethical issues in a professional manner. Additionally, it is imperative that they follow district and school policies and any legal precedents when handling any ethical issue.

Skill 3.4   Apply legal guidelines (e.g., in relation to students with disabilities, bilingual education, confidentiality, discrimination) to protect the rights of students and staff and to improve learning opportunities.

Once school principals have an understanding of the important issues affecting teaching and learning, they must deal with them using existing legal guidelines. These guidelines exist to protect the rights of students and staff.

The No Child Left Behind Act (NCLB) is one such guideline designed to help schools improve by focusing on accountability for results, freedom for states and communities, proven education methods, and parental choice. Some important terms associated with NCLB include adequate yearly progress (AYP), standardized assessments, and Title I.

Today in our country's schools there are over 6 million eligible children with disabilities. The Individuals with Disabilities Education Act (IDEA) was enacted in 1975 to ensure that children with disabilities have the opportunity to receive a free appropriate public education, equal in opportunity to that of other children. IDEA is in place to improve accountability, expand services, simplify parental involvement, and provide earlier access to services and supports for students with disabilities. There is a continuous goal of educating students with special needs in the least restrictive environment.

Each child with a disability has the right to educational services designed to meet his or her individual needs. Students receiving special and/or related services will be educated with general education students to the maximum extent appropriate to the needs of both. They will be integrated as much as possible in school activities and have access to an array of services, such as transportation, fine arts, physical education, counseling, and clubs. Educational and related services will be provided without cost to the special needs student except for those fees that are charged to general education students. Service(s) will be provided as close to the student's home as possible. When transportation to a more distant school or center is necessary, transportation will be provided at no cost to the parent.

The need for extended school year (ESY) services, the time between the end of one school year and the beginning of the next, is an IEP team decision. Students who have significant disabilities that are likely to continue for a prolonged period of time or indefinitely may require ESY services. ESY is required when the interruption of the student's specialized program will cause a loss of skills, which, when coupled with the limited recoupment capacity, makes it unlikely or impossible that the student will attain the level of self-sufficiency and independence that would otherwise be expected in view of his or her disability.

The U.S. population has changed dramatically in the past three decades, as nearly 30 million immigrants, both authorized and unauthorized, have settled here seeking a better future for themselves and their children. During the 2011–2012 school year, nearly 1 in 10—4.4 million—public school children received special assistance to learn English (Digest of Education Statistics 2012, table 204.20). This number continues to steadily increase. These students, like all others, are protected by Title VI of the Civil Rights Act. This act states: "school systems are responsible for assuring that students of a particular race, color, or national origin are not denied the opportunity to obtain the education generally obtained by other students in the system." Additionally, a section of the U.S. Equal Educational Opportunities Act (EEOC), the federal agency responsible for interpreting and enforcing Title VI, adds that each state is mandated to protect and help students "overcome language barriers that impede equal participation by its students in its instructional programs."

Maintaining confidentiality is of utmost importance in the school setting. Students, parents, or staff members must feel that important information is kept confidential to promote active participation in the school community. FERPA, the Family Educational Rights and Privacy Act, is a federal law that addresses confidentiality in the schools and governs the disclosure of student education records.

Skill 3.5   Apply laws, policies, and procedures in a fair and reasonable manner.

The current legal atmosphere is causing principals to act more cautiously and always consider the legal repercussions of issues with both students and staff. The threat of lawsuits affects decisions that are made every day. Principals who treat people fairly, implement policies and procedures consistently, and keep proper documentation should not feel threatened by the law. Additionally, effective principals will try to anticipate and prevent issues before they arise. When they do arise, teachers, students, and parents will be looking to the principal to make sure that situations are handled professionally and within the laws and guidelines. If your relationships with staff, students, and parents are open, honest, and consistent, the majority of issues can be resolved through conversation, instruction, and compromise.

Principals should first spend time researching laws, policies, and procedures that are most likely to affect them. Look for legal updates and state or district updates on policies and procedures on a regular basis. Stay informed about what laws have changed and about the practices and procedures that you might need to look at more carefully. Finally, take that information and disseminate it to the staff, students, and parents or other parties that should remain informed.

Skill 3.6   Articulate the importance of education in a free democratic society.

It is a widely known fact that nations with the highest level of secondary schooling are among the richest nations in the world. High rates of education are essential for countries to achieve high levels of economic growth. Education fosters our society's development. Additionally, we know that education allows people to move up in the world, seek better jobs, and ultimately succeed. In the United States, educational attainment is one of the top measures of social class.

The endeavors of a free democratic society depend on responsible, thoughtful, and innovative citizens. Educating students is a detailed, challenging task that requires a deep understanding of ethical principles, moral values, political theory, and economics. It also requires that educators have an understanding of who children are, both as individuals and as members of society.

Principals must not only ensure that curriculum contains information about becoming responsible citizens and that teachers are teaching this, but also model this behavior daily.

Skill 3.7   Serve as an advocate for all children.

An advocate is a person who speaks or writes in support or defense of a person or cause.

Principals have a responsibility to act as advocates for the children they serve every day. Parents place their children in the school's care. Parents and community members should view schools as their partners in education, not as separate entities.

Principals' number one priority is to make sure that children are in a safe and secure learning environment. With every decision principals make, they should ask themselves, "Is this in the best interest of the students?" If the answer to that question is No, they must be able to fight for what they believe is best.

Skill 3.8   Promote the continuous and appropriate development of all students.

Research confirms that among school-related variables, principals follow right behind teachers in shaping students' learning outcomes (Marzono, Waters, and McNulty, 2003). However, unlike teachers, who work directly with students, the influence of administrative leaders on student achievement is largely indirect (for example, hiring and supervising staff, creating a culture of high expectations, observing and giving feedback on instruction, establishing data systems that inform instructional decision making, working with staff to interpret and act on learning results). Through these indirect actions, principals establish the conditions that support student achievement. Principals must focus their school on how all children can have regular and sustained opportunities to learn and to achieve.

The change process at schools is notoriously slow, and principals who come into schools seeking immediate change may find themselves in a precarious position. Teachers are professionals with significant histories, cultures, and traditions. Many have been doing the same things for years, some with great success. Others have tried new ideas, have failed, and are fearful of doing anything new again. Therefore, principals who seek to change schools, introduce new curricula, or simply improve instructional quality must do so carefully and honestly. It is naïve to think that the introduction of another program or textbook or the addition of a new instructional technique will improve teaching and learning. Because schools are complex places, all changes are susceptible to failure or success, largely based on how those changes are received by stakeholders, including teachers, students, and parents.

Creating the kind of dynamic learning environments that twenty-first-century students need requires new approaches to teacher training. We want our children to become self-directed, goal-oriented, lifelong learners, and we can ask no less of those who teach them. Student needs and local goals drive all professional development from the inside out.

School change is often less about hoping teachers will adopt new ideas and more about forcing new ideas on teachers and schools. However, research shows that teachers may not fully adopt ideas they do not like. Therefore, whether change is imposed from above or encouraged by peers or leaders, motivation must be considered. Again, getting teachers involved in the planning and development process is critical to success.

As already stated, one primary reason teachers may be less willing to adopt new ideas is fear of failure. Instructional motivation, therefore, seeks to minimize the fears associated with adopting instructional innovations. Possible ways to do this include professional learning communities (in which teachers can come together to discuss instructional problems and solutions), lesson study (deliberate analysis of specific lessons in small groups of teachers), instructional coaches, and classroom observations (in which teachers are given time to watch other teachers teach).

Skill 3.9 Promote awareness of learning differences, multicultural awareness, gender sensitivity, and ethnic appreciation.

Principals are aware that a school with a variety of races, ethnicities, and learning differences can provide extraordinary academic and social opportunities to the entire school community. Diverse schools offer opportunities not always available in other settings. When knowledge can be shared not only by teachers and textbooks, but also by fellow students with a variety of life experiences and cultures, learning takes on new meaning. For example, classroom discussions with students from varying backgrounds can be rich and challenging, fostering critical thinking skills. Students learn there are different perspectives on global issues, motivating them to study and more thoughtfully define their own views.

It is important to make sure that everyone feels safe and comfortable in school. Try to make students and parents feel welcome and included in every aspect of the school community. Invite members of diverse groups to share their stories or cultures with others.

Principals must recognize and respect the diversity in their school. The key for effective school leaders in a diverse school is to face any obstacles early, tackle them with energy and creativity, and build a school culture based on a foundation of respect and high expectations. Creating awareness among the entire school community is an important step in the success of a diverse school. When doing this, principals should ensure that community stakeholders know that diversity is recognized and valued in their schools. Principals should offer resources, such as professional development, to help teachers and parents become more culturally aware. Additionally, principals should provide an environment in which all stakeholders are treated fairly and equitably.

COMPETENCY 4.0   THE PRINCIPAL KNOWS HOW TO FACILITATE THE DESIGN AND IMPLEMENTATION OF CURRICULA AND STRATEGIC PLANS THAT ENHANCE TEACHING AND LEARNING; ENSURE ALIGNMENT OF CURRICULUM, INSTRUCTION, RESOURCES, AND ASSESSMENT; AND PROMOTE THE USE OF VARIED ASSESSMENTS TO MEASURE STUDENT PERFORMANCE.

Skill 4.1   Facilitate effective campus curriculum planning based on knowledge of various factors (e.g., emerging issues, occupational and economic trends, demographic data, student learning data, motivation theory, teaching and learning theory, principles of curriculum design, human developmental processes, legal requirements).

For thousands of years, philosophers and psychologists have sought to understand and explain the nature of learning—how it occurs, and how one person can influence the learning of another person through teaching. Understanding the following theories can strengthen campus curriculum planning, but no one theory fits each school or classroom.

- Behaviorism: According to behaviorist theory, the learner is passive. We start with a clean slate, and behavior is shaped through positive or negative reinforcement. Behaviorists, like B. F. Skinner, believe that learning is a change of behavior caused by something that happens from the outside in.
- Cognitivism: Cognitivists, like Bruner, believe that people are not "programmed animals." Instead, the mind is like a computer: information comes in, the mind processes it, and this thinking leads to an outcome. Learning requires active participation, and behavior is changed as a result of thinking.
- Constructivism: Constructivism is the view that learning is an active, constructive process and that new learning is linked to prior knowledge. Humans are not a blank slate; they bring past experiences and cultural factors that influence learning. Vygotsky, Piaget, and Dewey were forerunners in this learning theory.
- Humanism: Humanism is the view that learning is student-centered and that the educator is simply a facilitator. Maslow and Carl Rogers were leading humanists, and their theory combines human motivation and the affective realm with the cognitive processes.
- 21st Century Skills: This is an education and standards movement that believes that the focus of learning should be on skill sets that will allow students to be successful in a future career. In addition to academic

subjects, students should be taught environmental literacy, health literacy, financial literacy, leadership, problem solving, information literacy, and global awareness.

There are some basic principles that underlie effective learning.

1. Students' prior knowledge can help or hinder learning. Students come into our courses with knowledge, beliefs, and attitudes gained in other courses and through daily life. As students bring this knowledge to bear in our classrooms, it influences how they filter and interpret what they are learning.
2. How students organize knowledge influences how they learn and apply what they know. Students naturally make connections among pieces of knowledge. When those connections form knowledge structures that are accurately and meaningfully organized, students are better able to retrieve and apply their knowledge effectively and efficiently. In contrast, when knowledge is connected in inaccurate or random ways, students can fail to retrieve or apply it appropriately.
3. Students' motivation determines, directs, and sustains what they do to learn. When students find value in a learning goal or activity, expect to achieve a desired learning outcome, and perceive support from their environment, they are likely to be strongly motivated to learn.
4. To develop mastery, students must acquire component skills, practice integrating them, and know when to apply what they have learned. Students must not only develop the component skills and knowledge necessary to perform complex tasks, but also practice combining and integrating them to develop greater fluency and automaticity.
5. Goal-directed practice coupled with targeted feedback enhances the quality of students' learning. Learning and performance are best fostered when students engage in practice that focuses on a specific goal or criterion, targets an appropriate level of challenge, and is of sufficient quantity and frequency to meet the performance criteria.
6. Students' current level of development interacts with the social, emotional, and intellectual climate of the course to impact learning. Students are not only intellectual but also social and emotional beings. While we cannot control the developmental process, we can shape the intellectual, social, emotional, and physical aspects of classroom climate in developmentally appropriate ways.
7. To become self-directed learners, students must learn to monitor and adjust their approaches to learning. Learners may engage in a variety of metacognitive processes to monitor and control their learning—assessing the task at hand, evaluating their strengths and weaknesses, planning their approach, applying and monitoring various strategies, and reflecting on the degree to which their current approach is working.

Instructional design is the process by which instruction is improved through the analysis of learning needs and systematic development of learning materials. Program effectiveness can be measured only through the process of evaluation. Program evaluation is the process of collecting and analyzing data to discover whether the design, development, or implementation is producing the desired outcomes. The data gathering and analyses are necessary for making informed decisions about the program, and they may lead to changing or eliminating aspects of the program.

The CIPP (Content, Input, Process, Product) model developed by Daniel Stufflebeam is one example of program evaluation. Information for decisions is provided in a three-step process, which includes delineating the information to be collected, obtaining the information, and providing the information to others. These steps correspond with four distinct types of evaluation: content, input, process, and product evaluations (Ornstein and Hunkins, 1993). *Content evaluation* is concerned with the environment of the program in terms of needs and unmet needs. *Context evaluation* constitutes the diagnostic stage of the evaluative process. It provides baseline information related to the entire system of operation. *Input evaluation* is concerned with providing information and determining how to utilize resources to attain the goals of the program. It focuses on whether the goals and objectives for the program are appropriate to the expected outcome or if the goals and objectives are stated appropriately. It also takes into account whether the resources to implement specific strategies are adequate, whether the strategies are appropriate to attain the goals, or if the time allotted is appropriate to meet the objectives set forth for the program.

Process evaluation focuses on decisions regarding curriculum implementation. It is concerned with whether the activities planned are being implemented and with the logistics of the total operation so that procedures are recorded as they occur and monitoring is continuous to identify potential problems. The continuous process of identifying potential problems leads to decisions to make corrections before or during the implementation of the program. For example, it might be necessary to establish special planning sessions or teacher in-service at specific grade levels to work on modification of some of the strategies established for the program because of problems that are uncovered. Process evaluation is also known as the piloting process prior to the actual implementation of a school-wide or district-wide program (Ornstein and Hunkins, 1993). Finally, *product evaluation* takes into account whether, and to what degree, the final product or curriculum is accomplishing the goals or objectives.

At this point, decisions must be made regarding the continuation, termination, or modification of the program. Since the evaluation process is continuous, at this point the evaluators may link specific actions to other stages of the cycle or make changes based on the data collected. The data obtained may indicate the need to delay full implementation of the program until corrections are made, or it may lead to the decision that the program is ready for large-scale implementation.

In summary, the main purposes of the evaluative process are to diagnose strengths and weaknesses and to provide feedback to make appropriate decisions for programs and schools. The data for the evaluation process originates from a number of sources, including classroom observation, interviews and discussions with students, discussion with teachers and parents, testing and measurement data, information from pupil services or guidance services, and surveys of the school and school community.

Systematic assessment of school needs may range from grade-level surveys of needs to school-wide surveys. This practice is insignificant unless careful attention is given to a cohesive set of goals that are developed collaboratively with administrators, teachers, parents, and members of the school community to address specific needs. It is important that the instrument gathers pertinent information related to students' needs and the program situation at the school. Once the instrument is administered and the results are quantified, analyzed, and interpreted, the direction to follow is determined.

When the purpose of the needs assessment is program development, goal statements are carefully established, and goals are prioritized and linked to performance outcomes of the learner. High-priority goals are placed into a plan of implementation with specific strategies delineated. However, if the purpose of the assessment is a progress check, the assessment instrument should reflect statements concerning activities and functions of the students and the staff and communication among the various levels. The systematic assessment of school needs should go beyond surveys to include cumulative folder content, anecdotal records, test results, interviews, classroom sociograms, direct teacher observation, and other means deemed appropriate.

Change is often necessary for growth and development, but not all change is accepted. In many instances, the acceptance of change depends on concrete measures of comparison between the existing and the desired programs. Such comparison might be done through the Provus Discrepancy Evaluation Model, in which program standards and performance are determined, and then performance and standards are compared to determine if there are discrepancies. The discrepancy between standards and performance is established throughout every aspect of the program, including the design, installation, processes, products, and cost.

When change is necessary, it will not occur just because someone has a great idea that may be beneficial and work beautifully. Change will occur when the individuals at all levels in the organization recognize that there is a need for it. It takes effective leadership and open two-way communication to initiate the change process. Problem solving, support, and continuous assessment of the process are also important aspects of promoting change.

The process of educating students is accomplished through instruction designed to attain specific objectives reflected in the educational aims and goals. Change occurs because the principal, curriculum leaders, teachers, parents, staff, and students work together and accept their roles as agents of change. The organizational pattern and climate must be transformed to accept change.

See also Skill 1.5 and Skill 3.5.

Skill 4.2   Facilitate the use of sound, research-based practice in the development, implementation, and evaluation of campus curricular, co-curricular, and extracurricular programs.

Curriculum and instructional materials are integral parts of a public school system. The school curriculum is an action plan to educate children. The aims and goals that shape education are generated from nationwide commissions and task forces comprised of educators and other influential citizens, including politicians. For example, the Commission on Excellence in Education prompted change when it reported on the quality of American education and made specific recommendations in its 1983 Nation at Risk report. Another example is the work of President Clinton and the governors of the states with the Goals 2000 effort, which emerged in 1993. For example, goal four of Goals 2000 states that "By the year 2000, U.S. students will be first in the world in science and mathematics achievement." The expectations of this societal goal affected the curriculum in every state, district, and school. Even if this goal is lofty and may never be attained, it has affected the selection and content of the local curriculum. National concerns about reading comprehension, math achievement, and science achievement affect curriculum selection in light of economic competition with other countries.

The State Board of Education periodically updates the state's curriculum standards, called the Texas Essential Knowledge and Skills (TEKS). It details the curriculum requirements for every course. The TEKS are taught to students, and student progress is measured, beginning in grade 3, with a state-mandated test based on these standards called the State of Texas Assessments of Academic Readiness (STAAR).

At the local level, task forces of parents, educators, and community groups impact school curriculum changes in similar ways as nationwide groups. Data sources to affect change at the local level sometimes include attitudinal surveys of the students, parent groups, teachers, and other community groups. Other data sources for curriculum selection include direct student information, such as interviews and conferences, which yield information related to disposition for learning, likes and dislikes, and difficulties students experience because of curriculum design or other related situations.

Research findings about curriculum principles and design and content organization also are valuable information for decision making. Sources for curriculum selection reflect the expectations of society, and they directly impact the objectives for learning. Because society is concerned with producing citizens who are prepared to transmit the ideals of a democratic society, the school as a social institution must include objectives that will produce learner outcomes that serve this purpose.

The design of the curriculum determines how the elements of the curriculum are organized. The design must account for the nature and organization of the aims, goals, and objectives, as well as the subject matter, learning activities, and evaluation. Curriculum design precedes instructional design. It is concerned with the nature of the component parts and is influenced by various philosophies, theories, and practical issues.

The designer must specify the nature of each of the elements included in the design to develop a blueprint before initiating the process of implementation. The goals and objectives should be specific so that all those involved will understand what will be done and what behaviors are expected of the learner. The next step is to identify the resources needed to attain the preset goals and objectives for the curriculum. All necessary materials and human resources must be identified and secured. Materials include textbooks, charts, maps, and other technology and equipment, such as projectors, computers, calculators, sports equipment, and microscopes. Human resources include administrators, teachers, volunteers, support staff, and others. Facilities are classrooms, gyms, athletic fields, cafeteria, auditoriums, and others. The subject matter, methods of organization, and activities, as well as the methods and instruments to evaluate the program, must be determined.

The conceptual framework, or the organization of curriculum components, consists of two organizational dimensions: horizontal and vertical. *Horizontal organization* is a side-by-side course arrangement in which the content of one subject is made relevant to the concepts of another related subject. *Vertical organization* is concerned with longitudinal treatment of concepts within a subject across grade levels. The success of the horizontal organization depends on the collaboration of teachers of various disciplines at the grade level, while the success of the vertical organization depends on collaboration and planning among teachers of various grade levels.

The dimensions within the curriculum content are also important. Attention should be given to curriculum scope, sequence, integration, continuity, articulation, and balance. *Curriculum scope* is the breadth and depth of the curriculum content at any grade level in terms of the content, learning activities and experiences, and topics. *Curriculum sequence* is the order of topics to be studied over time in a vertical dimension. The sequence of the curriculum is usually from simple to complex learning, but it also can emphasize chronological learning, whole to part learning, or prerequisite learning. *Curriculum integration* is the linking of the concepts, skills, and experiences in the subjects taught.

Curriculum continuity is the spiral or vertical smoothness with which subject content is repeated from one grade level to the next. *Curriculum articulation* is the relationships within and among subjects both vertically and horizontally. *Curriculum balance* is opportunities for learners to master knowledge and apply it in their personal, social, and intellectual pursuits.

The school curriculum should satisfy societal needs and specific goals to produce an individual who has the social, intellectual, moral, emotional, and civic development to function as an integral part of our democratic society. Considering this, selecting the best curriculum to meet all of these needs is a difficult task and should be a collaborative effort. A response to why program changes are necessary should provide a clear rationale that examines the existing district and school goals. It should clarify subject structure and content and the needs of the students regarding ability, performance, level of success, and strategies. Motivation of students and instructional staff; feasibility of time and resources; and curriculum balance in terms of concepts, skills, and application should also be considered.

Successful curriculum implementation is dependent on careful planning, and communication during the implementation process is pivotal, especially when the new curriculum will upset the status quo. The channels of communication must always be open so that discussions and exchange are ongoing at all levels and across groups. Effective communication requires high-quality exchange through two-way channels within a defined network. While the formal network remains the official way of communicating in organizations, the informal network should not be ignored or discouraged because it can be shaped into a healthy system of communication among members of the organization.

Curriculum implementation requires that administrators and support personnel not only understand the curriculum, but also provide classroom support to meet needs. Therefore, the communication model must be responsive to the needs of all involved. Effective lateral communication allows information flow among all participants at varying levels of involvement in the curriculum while valuing their contributions and promoting involvement through the process of networking. Lateral communication is usually formal within the organization, yet informal channels tend to be lateral as well. Examples of informal lateral communication are a small group of teachers deciding to get together and share ideas from an article that could be useful with certain children in their classroom, or the development of a simulation project for the grade level. Formal lateral communication messages may be written and disseminated in a systematic way through newsletters, bulletin, memos, and reports.

A needs assessment is always the initial step in program planning. It provides the opportunity to survey and identify the context in which the program will be developed. The needs assessment survey should focus on the needs of the students to identify the achievement problems, write the goals for the initial planning stage, and formulate specific objectives for instruction.

Identifying the educational goals and setting priorities before developing the curriculum are essential aspects of planning. Additionally, setting and prioritizing the goals must be carefully linked to learners' performance. The design of the curriculum follows with the careful selection and recommendation of instructional materials and equipment and methods to attain the pre-established goals and objectives. The next steps include the organization of the personnel involved and the implementation of a plan to supervise and give direction and focus to the project. Finally, the product planning and implementation at the classroom level are followed by the evaluation process, which determines the effectiveness and attainment of the goals and objectives of the curriculum.

The implementation process must be strategically planned with benchmarks to determine specific levels of program goal attainment, leading to the reexamination of the strategies being used for specific learning outcomes. When placed on a time line, the benchmarks may also serve as indicators for communicating with various stakeholders. Feedback from audiences must be used to determine the extent to which curriculum goals and expected outcomes, content, and implementation strategies, as well as outcome measures, are understood. The plan will supply the agenda items that will be acted on in a timely manner and hence drive the implementation process and the dissemination process.

In the process of educational program evaluation or classroom instructional evaluation, outcomes are reflected in terms of aims, goals, and objectives. Aims are general statements that reflect value judgments that give overall direction to the curriculum. They guide the educational process to achieve future behavioral outcomes. Aims are the results of societal concerns, which usually are expressed through national commissions and task forces. Goals are more specific than aims.

Even though goals may be written in a general manner similar to aims, aims become goals when the statement of purpose reflects a specific area of the curriculum. Objectives are the most specific statements of expected learner outcomes. Examples of goals are expressed in the 1993 national Goals 2000. Goal one states, "By the year 2000 all children in America will start school ready to learn." Goal two states, "By the year 2000 the high school graduation rate will increase."

As observed, these goal statements are very general, and they do not include specific behaviors or terms for the behavior. Objectives are generally expressed in behavioral terms, which are measurable. Nonbehavioral objectives are generally used to express higher-order learning, suggesting such nonquantifiable measurement as appreciation and understanding. In most schools, behavioral objectives are preferred to nonbehavioral objectives. Behavioral objectives state what is expected of the student at the conclusion of the unit or lesson. They state the terms for the behavior and the minimum expectancy. For example: After completing the unit on telling time, students will be able to complete 25 problems with 80% accuracy within a 30-minute time span.

From the onset of the program, the goals and objectives are vital. The identified problems are addressed through the goals and objectives. Goals and objectives should be clearly written and examined to make sure that they represent expectations. To obtain buy-in and ownership in the attainment of the goals and objectives, parents, students, staff, and other members of the school community must be included in the process. Objectives should be written in measurable terms, and because they are specific, special attention should be given to the behavior to be measured, the situation in which the performance will take place, and the criterion for the performance. For example, students will be able to solve multiplication word problems (behavior) at the rate of one problem per minute (situation) with 80% accuracy (condition). Objectives can be written to give directions at various program levels, including grade levels and subject levels.

In addition to curriculum delivered through courses in schools, the principal must manage extracurricular and co-curricular activities, which can be used to acquire valuable skills. These include the following:

- The specific skills being practiced in the extracurricular. For instance, playing the violin for your school orchestra makes you better at playing the violin and helps you appreciate music better, and you might be able to tutor others in the violin later in life.
- General skills related to hard work, perseverance, concentration, and acquisition of mastery.
- Skills related to dealing with people. Many extracurricular activities involve activities that rely on teamwork. Some involve dealing with customers or potential customers, and some involve understanding what other people are thinking.

Skill 4.3 Facilitate campus participation in collaborative district planning, implementation, monitoring, and revision of curriculum to ensure appropriate scope, sequence, content, and alignment.

In this age of school accountability, principals are indeed instructional leaders. They must be responsible for the quality of instruction on their campuses. While they cannot be fully responsible, because schools are made up of many professionals, they have great influence on the instruction in each classroom.

In terms of curriculum, decisions are often made at the district level or within departments or committees. School leaders generally defer to the expertise of teachers or curriculum specialists; however, they can have a strong impact on procedures, standards, and outcomes. By being present, staying informed, and working collaboratively, they can help create high-level curriculum for all classrooms.

Where does curriculum come from? It originates in the purposes of education that the community, board, state, or region hold dear. For example, when local stakeholders believe that all students should have strong knowledge of civic foundations, developing a curriculum for teaching civics is the most pertinent next step. Schools are unlikely to develop curriculum for academic areas that are not important to any stakeholder group. When appropriate topics are determined, curriculum is developed to organize the content into a manageable and logical progression. Curriculum usually is organized by topic areas; added to those topics are texts, outside resources, assessments, projects, and activities. Additionally, specific instructional techniques are recommended.

Usually curricula are already developed for most subjects. Why is curriculum still an issue, then? Primarily because all curriculum can be improved. Most schools modify curriculum on a regular basis. They draw from previous experience of what worked and what didn't work. Additionally, when new priorities are handed down to schools (in the form of legislation, for example), schools want to create a curriculum that will reflect their individual needs even though the basic structures may be in place already. In such cases, pieces of the curriculum are adapted. Sources, such as conferences, books, programs, and formal interventions, are helpful in creating curriculum.

Instructional objectives are met primarily though trial, feedback, improvement, and new knowledge. Teachers cannot teach better without new ideas, practice, and advice. Principals and other teacher leaders, instructional coaches, and mentors can provide valuable assistance to teachers as they seek to improve their practice. This brings up an important point: Effective resources for teachers include sources of new knowledge; however, one-on-one coaching or mentoring is particularly effective in helping teachers improve. Although principals can be effective at this, teachers may trust nonevaluative staff more with questions, concerns, or problems that they need addressed.

Whatever the process, a clear relationship among goals, activities, and students' assessment is established. Collaborative curriculum planning and decision making is the typical method. Curriculum continuity is built across grade levels, programs, and courses. Curriculum alignment is periodic, and staff, students, and parents know the priorities of the scope of the curriculum. The content of the curriculum is free from biases, including gender, ethnic, and racial biases.

The school curriculum is a plan of action to educate children. The plan includes goals and objectives, activities for learning, materials to support learning, and the evaluation process to determine the attainment of the goals and objectives. This plan is placed into a design that is undergirded by the selected approach and philosophy of learning. There are many different approaches to curriculum. These approaches are a reflection of educational philosophies, psychological foundations, and social and developmental theories. Approaches to curriculum also include viewpoints about curriculum design; the roles of the learners, teachers, and specialists; goals and objectives; and other important content to be examined.

Curriculum approaches can be technical scientific or nontechnical/nonscientific. Among the technical scientific approaches are specific behavioral approaches, the managerial approach, and the systems approach. Among the nontechnical/nonscientific approaches to curriculum are the academic approaches and the humanistic approaches.

The behavioral approach, pioneered by Ralph Tyler, Franklin Babbit, Hilda Tabba, and others, provides an efficient model to run schools. It is a blueprint that includes goals and objectives, step-by-step sequencing of content, activities, and learning outcome. This approach is rooted in the scientific management theory of Frederick Taylor, which emphasizes efficiency and productivity; its legacy is still observed in teacher lesson plans and units.

The managerial approach considers the school as a social system in which students, teachers, administrators, and other members of the school community interact based on certain social norms. In this setting, space, schedules, and programs are important factors. While logical and sequential steps are expected, the focus is on the organizational aspect of curriculum rather than the implementation. This approach brought about innovations, such as nongraded schools, departmentalization, the homeroom concept, and others. Its main goal is to organize the curriculum into a system.

The system approach views units and subunits of organization as integral parts of the whole. Diagrams and flow charts are important to view the curriculum as a whole system that can be monitored. The system approach is considered curriculum engineering. In this approach, particular issues are related to the whole system in terms of the relationship of the entire program.

The academic approach is among the nonscientific/nontechnical approaches to curriculum. It is philosophical and theoretical and is especially concerned with broad aspects of schooling and background information. Its overview of events and people make it rigid and impractical for the classroom and schools. Nonetheless, it includes useful educational views for curriculum developers and theorists.

The humanistic approach is another nonscientific/nontechnical approach rooted in the child-centered movement, which gained recognition with the growth of child psychology and humanistic psychology in the 1940s and 1950s. This approach is concerned with the social, artistic, physical, and cultural aspects of curriculum. Additionally, it is concerned with the need for learner self-reflection and self-actualization, along with the social and psychological environmental dynamics of the classroom.

Educational philosophies provide the primary foundation on which educators build the curriculum. Philosophies reflect a particular school of thought and provide the impetus for the aims, goals, content, and organization of the curriculum. Educational philosophies provide educators with a basis for school and classroom organization. They provide information related to methodology, materials for instruction, content, experiences, and other structural issues related to the teaching and learning process.

Skill 4.4   Facilitate the use of appropriate assessments to measure student learning and ensure educational accountability.

School administrators must implement appropriate assessments to measure individual student growth during the school year and from year to year, rather than measuring student achievement at a single point in time. Implementing a system of assessment ensures that teachers and administrators can understand and influence growth for all students, regardless of achievement status, age, or class groupings. Analyzing these growth measures over time will also help determine how student achievement is aligned with district or state standards. Teachers should also be able to determine if classroom instruction is challenging individual students appropriately.

Teachers must be encouraged to shift from assessment *of* learning to assessment *for* learning. Assessment for learning is the process of seeking and interpreting evidence for use by learners and their teachers to decide where the learners are in their learning, where they need to go, and how best to get there (http://www.aaia.org.uk/pdf/AFL_10principlesARG.pdf). Assessment for learning is an ongoing process, whereas assessment of learning is done at a point in time for the purpose of summarizing the current status of student achievement.

Additionally, research shows that assessment is most effective when it includes the following characteristics:
- Student centered
- Congruent with instructional objectives
- Relevant
- Comprehensive
- Clear (in purpose, directions, expectations)
- Objective and fair
- Simulates end behavior/product/performance
- Incites active responses
- Shows progress/development over time

Skill 4.5   Facilitate the use of technology, telecommunications, and information systems to enrich the campus curriculum.

A 2013 survey of K–12 teachers in the United States shows that close to 74% of all teachers surveyed said they use digital resources—such as tablets and computers—to expand on and reinforce content in their classrooms. (PBSlearningmedia.org). Among the other highlights: 69% of those surveyed said educational technology helps them "do much more than ever before" for their students, with the most commonly used resources being online lesson plans, interactive web games, and online articles.

Without a doubt, technology helps increase academic achievement. Organizations like Edutopia, the North Central Educational Lab (NCREL), and the Center for Applied Research in Educational Technology (CARET) are studying and tracking how technology is increasing academic achievement. Students today do not learn the same way as students did in the twentieth century. Technology has taken over their lives, and using it in the classroom can create enthusiasm and better learning outcomes and sustain interest in all subject areas in academics.

Schools use information systems to enhance learning through dynamic educational software developments, ranging from games to virtual field trips. According to studies, educational software designers have developed games that improve student motivation, promote constructivist and collaborative learning, and improve academic learning (*Computers & Education*, v52 n1 pp. 68–77, Jan. 2009).

E-learning, Web CT, online classes, and distance learning are classified as forms of instructional technology. There are numerous distance learning benefits, including the following:

- This technology enables students to attend classes when situations do not permit them to attend the on-campus classroom.
- Online courses give students flexibility to work on assignments when their schedule permits them. This releases students from attending a class on a set day and time.
- It enables students to do interactive teamwork. Students have the opportunity to correspond with others from different backgrounds and to hear from a variety of speakers from around the world.

The possibilities of learning with information systems is endless. Students are able to use the Internet for research. They can create multimedia presentations in all subject areas. Students of all ages can use online activities that pertain to their subject matter. Keyboarding skills can be developed at very early ages, even before kindergarten. To live and learn in an information-rich society, students must be able to use technology effectively in an educational setting and beyond.

The use of technology in teaching can help with many of the expectations teachers faced. Technology allows students to have reference materials at their fingertips. The Web is not only a source of communication but also a reference for an enormous number of topics. The Internet includes videos that enable visual learners to study topics in a way that they process information best. One example is Discovery Education, where just about any topic can be found and used in the classroom. This resource provides educators with engaging digital resources to be more effective in the classroom and increase student interest by connecting the classroom to information from around the world. When using such resources, the teacher becomes facilitator in learning the subject material rather than a lecturer presenting materials.

Other instructional technology tools that teachers can present to students include the following:

- Concept maps: This type of software enables students to work individually or in groups to create graphical representations of knowledge. Students retain information using various learning styles.
- Online test repositories like Exam View or QuizStar enable students to take tests online and receive reports immediately. Teachers receive reports that show them where students are struggling much sooner than pen/paper unit tests of the past.

Collaboration among teachers can occur if lessons are stored in a centralized location in a database or on a server. This allows teachers to borrow lessons that will improve students' performance on a particular topic. The use of this type of information technology can strengthen education by enabling teachers to share expertise.

In the past, parents did not see students' grades until progress time or a report card was sent home. Many schools now have the capability to allow parents to view their child's grades online. Using school information systems allows parents to see their child's grades, assignments, and tests. This collaboration between teachers and parents helps students succeed.

The thrust to use technology in the learning environment is not likely to abate in the near future. So, for school administrators, it is important to recognize the capabilities of technology and the advantages it brings to the classroom, as well as becoming an advocate for using technology. A major responsibility falls on the school leader to model technology use and to also provide access and training for teachers to use technology.

The use of technology in schools by teachers and students is contingent on an understanding of the capabilities of various technologies and an ability to integrate these capabilities into the curriculum framework of a school. The application of technology to curriculum goals and objectives is an important function of school leadership. Involving students in learning sequences that utilize technology provides a new and motivating context to learning. Proponents of technology assert a significant role for technology in the teaching and learning process. They view technology as an ingredient with potential to transform the relationship between students and teachers and the dynamics that take place in the classroom. Computer technology offers teachers and students a constructivist learning environment, an opportunity for students to engage in hands-on learning.

Skill 4.6 Facilitate the effective coordination of campus curricular, co-curricular and extracurricular programs in relation to other district programs

Co-curricular refers to activities, programs, and learning experiences that complement, in some way, what students are learning in school; for example, experiences that are connected to or mirror the academic curriculum.

Co-curricular activities are typically, but not always, defined by their separation from academic courses. For example, they are ungraded, they do not allow students to earn academic credit, they may take place outside school or after regular school hours, and they may be operated by outside organizations.

A few examples of common educational opportunities that may be considered co-curricular include student newspapers; musical performances; art shows; mock trials; debate competitions; and mathematics, robotics, and engineering teams and contests. But given the differing interpretations of the term and its many potential applications, it's best to determine precisely how *co-curricular* is being used in a particular educational context.

Co-curricular vs. Extracurricular

Generally speaking, co-curricular activities are an extension of the formal learning experiences in a course or academic program, while extracurricular activities may be offered or coordinated by a school but may not be explicitly connected to academic learning. This distinction is fuzzy in practice, however, and the terms are often used interchangeably. Athletics, for example, are typically considered extracurricular activities, while a science fair would more likely be considered a co-curricular activity because students are learning science, participation may be required by the school, students may be graded on their entries, or a science teacher may coordinate the fair.

Skill 4.7 **Promote the use of creative thinking, critical thinking and problem solving by staff and other campus stakeholders involved in curriculum design and delivery**

The process of curriculum development is social, political, and historical. It involves an ongoing process of orientation, moving from personal sense-making to reference to departmental, institutional, and national norms.

Beginning in the 1990s, constructivist theory began to gain traction, and its influence on instructional design became more prominent as a counterpoint to the more traditional cognitive learning theory. Constructivists believe that learning experiences should be authentic and produce real-world learning environments that allow learners to construct their own knowledge. This emphasis on the learner was a significant departure from traditional forms of instructional design.

Another trend that surfaced during this period was the recognition of performance improvement as an important outcome of learning that needed to be considered during the design process.

Other influences on curriculum design include the following:

- The World Wide Web has become a learning tool.
- As technology advanced and constructivist theory gained popularity, technology's use in the classroom evolved from mostly drill-and-skill exercises to more interactive activities that require more complex thinking on the part of the learner.
- Rapid prototyping was first seen during the 1990s. In this process, an instructional design project is prototyped quickly and then vetted through a series of try and revise cycles. This is a big departure from traditional methods of instructional design that took far longer to complete.

The 2000s: Rise of the Internet and Online Learning

The Internet, with its social media tools and information resources, has become a very popular tool for online learning, and instructional designers have recognized the need to integrate e-learning into learning objects and curricula. There has been a great increase in the number of online courses offered by higher education institutions.

Technology has advanced to the point that sophisticated simulations are now readily available to learners, providing more authentic and realistic learning experiences.

2010 and Forward

The influence of e-tools continues to grow and has encouraged the growth of informal learning throughout a person's lifetime. The challenge for instructional designers is how to create learning opportunities that can occur anywhere and anytime.

Curriculum design rarely starts from a blank slate; instead, curriculum designers draw on existing courses, texts, and web resources and on their own experience and understanding to shape a course. Inheriting courses in which the context and the method of assessment are fixed can be stifling. Nonetheless, teachers are expected to take ownership of the course and make it their own. Teachers can create new understandings of a previously unfamiliar area, improvise in response to students' experiences, and negotiate the content and process to some extent. Such creativity involves calling into question what's always been taught. This is particularly difficult when dealing with high-stakes assessments. In an environment in which failure is unacceptable, teachers will tend to avoid risk and eschew innovation in favor of safe, predictable lessons.

COMPETENCY 5.0   **THE PRINCIPAL KNOWS HOW TO ADVOCATE, NURTURE, AND SUSTAIN AN INSTRUCTIONAL PROGRAM AND A CAMPUS CULTURE THAT ARE CONDUCIVE TO STUDENT LEARNING AND STAFF PROFESSIONAL GROWTH.**

Skill 5.1   **Facilitate the development of a campus learning organization that supports instructional improvement and change through ongoing study of relevant research and best practice.**

Schools, teachers, principals, students, and parents all feel the push for higher standards and for better performance on standardized tests. Yet, most teachers did not go into the profession to help students pass tests; most students are not very motivated by multiple-choice exams; most parents value other forms of assessment; and most principals do not want to see their campus communities stressed out over these issues. The tests are here to stay, and students, teachers, principals, and schools will continue to be assessed based on achievement levels.

In the research on schools as organizations over the past two decades, significant accomplishments have been made in characterizing teachers as professionals, schools as learning communities, and educational work as complex. The more we see teachers as professionals who can make decisions regarding their work in the classroom, even if they must follow prescribed curriculum, the more they are willing to demonstrate commitment to their work. This is important for many reasons.

First, considering that teachers, principals, and schools are asked to utilize assessment data more frequently to make instructional decisions, principals need to provide a climate and context in which to do so. For example, say that a teacher is told that he must use assessment data to make instructional decisions, but then is provided a curriculum to follow and told not to deviate from it. Is this teacher going to feel that his instructional decisions will be valued? What happens when this teacher notices a problem that needs to be addressed, and the curriculum provides no assistance for that particular problem? Do the messages from the school indicate that the teacher's first priority is the curriculum? If so, when problems arise, will the teacher be willing to expend energy to find solutions?

Second, if teachers feel supported in making decisions based on data, do they have the resources and tools with which to do so? Many critics argue that teachers who have entered school systems prior to the huge emphasis on data use will struggle more with making instructional decisions based on assessment results. Principals, staff developers, and teacher leaders must provide assistance and motivation so that all faculty feel supported in this new and complex challenge.

Third, when teachers are committed to their work as professionals, they see greater value in learning new instructional techniques and experimenting with assessment ideas. Learning new approaches to teaching takes significant time—and it also opens up teachers to a host of problems when something does not work right in the classroom. As professionals, teachers need to feel safe with experimenting with new approaches to teaching, and they need multiple avenues for feedback and assistance.

So, how do principals create communities of professionals in their schools? How do they help teachers become more committed to their work in their classrooms? Many people would argue that schools have to encounter cultural shifts that allow professional discussions not only to take place, but also to be demanded by teachers. Typically, professional discussion about student learning and teacher techniques is said to take place in professional learning communities (PLCs). PLCs take many different forms, but they all have one thing in common: teachers working as professionals to problem solve, participate in dialogues, and question instructional strategies. For example, some PLCs operate through reading groups. In reading groups, teachers select professional books to read and discuss, typically on a monthly basis. A group of English teachers might select a new publication about student portfolios, read the book on their own, and then discuss both the content of the book and the possible applications of the book to the school and to each of their classrooms.

Another common format for PLCs is group scoring sessions. Let's say a group of grade 10 social studies teachers assign their students a similar end-of-unit writing project. They utilize the same assignment, have the same standards, and assess the work according to the same rubric. As a group, the teachers can score these essays together, discussing similar problems they notice, seeking help from one another on making sense of quality, and brainstorming solutions so that they can better prepare students for the next assessment.

The list of options for PLCs is extensive. Any format is possible, as long as it focuses teachers on student learning. The trick of making PLCs work is for teachers to feel supported as professionals in all aspects of their work—not just in these PLC settings.

| **Skill 5.2** | **Facilitate the implementation of sound, research-based instructional strategies, decisions, and programs in which multiple opportunities to learn and be successful are available to all students.** |

Effective teachers plan for instructional delivery even if they have taught the same lessons before. They continue to improve their presentation by finding new or additional materials that bring new energy to the teaching and learning. As part of teaching, planning is a deliberate act that can be long range or short range, formal or informal. Long-range planning, such as units or semester plans, takes into account milestones, standards, and major goals over a period of time. It takes into account the nature of the content to be covered, the process through which the content will be covered, the approaches to take at varying stages, the activities to be used, and the resources needed. Short-term planning consists of daily lesson plans and weekly—or even monthly—plans or units for instruction. Daily and weekly lesson plans are usually more detailed and specific, while unit plans can be more general and serve as the source of the daily lesson plans. Daily, weekly, and unit written plans; grouping of students; instructional materials selection; activities for specific experiences to attain specific goals; student assessment; and the like are all part of the planning process.

The formal aspect of planning has greater breadth and scope, which includes long-term and short-term written plans. The informal aspect of planning is continuous and includes teachers' ideas that emerge (1) as they gather materials they believe will be useful for learning, (2) as they consider varying experiences that could be used for specific students, (3) as they share ideas with other professionals, and (4) as they consider ideas on how to do things better. Whether long term or short term, effective planning begins with a goals and objectives specification for learning. Once the goals and objectives are specified, instructional strategies and materials should be selected, followed by the appropriate evaluation techniques to assess learning.

Instructional planning also involves organizing the students for learning. Whole-group and small-group instruction are beneficial in different ways. Whole-group instruction is beneficial when the teacher is introducing new concepts and skills; small-group instruction is recommended when teachers want to ensure that the students master the material or that thorough learning has taken place. Students may be placed in ability groups for short-term activities. Long-term ability grouping, such as tracking, should be avoided to allow children who would have been placed in regular track and those who would have been placed in college-bound track to benefit from one another by learning together.

Generally, teachers believe that ability groups save time and enable them to focus on the specific collective needs of the students. However, approaches such as cooperative groups, in which students of mixed ability work together, result in higher academic achievement at all levels of schooling. Other benefits include improved time on task and increased interpersonal skills. Cooperative grouping as a dominant approach to instruction does not negate the need to use, on a short-term basis, homogeneous groupings to work with children within the classroom. The teacher must be careful that short-term ability groups remain as such and that the lower groups still receive high-quality instruction.

Instruction should be clear and focused, beginning with an orientation to the lesson and instructional objectives presented to students in a language that they can easily understand. The relationship between the current lesson and previous lessons should be made. Key points should be emphasized, concepts defined with examples and nonexamples, cause and effect relationships established, and careful attention given to learning styles through the use of appropriate materials and strategies for learning. Students should be provided ample time for guided and independent practice in the form of class work and homework, and they should be given strategies to develop higher-level thinking skills.

Effective teacher expressions are critical to verbal instructional delivery. Enthusiasm and challenges that are clearly articulated are as important as the instruction itself. Instruction, demonstrated through body language that expresses interest and caring, also may contribute to verbal effectiveness. The teacher should use good verbal skills for effective questioning to monitor understanding, keep students focused, and give feedback to reinforce learning progress.

Skill 5.3   Create conditions that encourage staff, students, families/caregivers, and the community to strive to achieve the campus vision.

Principals must continually nurture a school climate that focuses on achieving the vision that the campus believes is most important. Many schools, in addition to working toward higher achievement on standardized tests, want students to be able to access and apply research from a variety of sources. Other schools are concerned with developing caring and responsible citizens. These goals should not be passed over for the sake of achievement tests. In many ways, the more we work to encourage the things in which we really believe, the more motivated the campus community will be to succeed in the other areas.

How do we create a campus climate that encourages staff, students, families, and the community to work toward specific, deeply held goals? There are many ways, all of which center on the importance of providing stakeholders with a voice.

In the 1990s, it was common for schools to develop site-based management committees. These teams were comprised of teachers, administrators, and possibly parents and students. The teams collectively made policy decisions for their campuses. Some districts purposely included parents and other community members on these teams and allowed them greater flexibility in designing policies for schools. Some even were given privileges for personnel decisions. Many of these teams have dissolved—based in part on a lack of evidence for their effectiveness and criticism of the political elements involved—but many still exist.

Current thinking on stakeholder voice in public schools is that all stakeholders should be able to see how decisions are made (through very transparent processes) and should be given multiple opportunities for comment and critique. Because schools are so heavily involved in a family's life (parents entrust schools to care for their children for approximately six hours per day), providing parents, especially, with open, transparent rationales for decisions is critical. Furthermore, policies and decisions should take parent and student concerns and needs seriously. The more parents feel accepted, the more they will see their place in the system.

Teachers also need to feel that they have a voice. Teachers want to be considered professionals, but when administrators take advantage of them or leave them out of critical decisions, they feel as if their levels of expertise are not valued. While their needs cannot always be met fully, the more administrators show them that their concerns are important, the more they will accept the rationales for decisions with which they are not happy.

Finally, beyond helping stakeholder groups see that a school values them, it is critical that a mission and vision be front and center in the daily operations of the school. A vision cannot be simply something that is written on a banner and hung in a hallway. It has to be talked about, referred to, and considered regularly, especially when decisions must be made.

Even though each stakeholder group sees its own interests as most important, these strategies provide principals with tools to break down barriers between groups as they seek to shape school culture.

Skill 5.4 Ensure that all students are provided high-quality, flexible instructional programs with appropriate resources and services to meet individual student needs.

Even though new principals often inherit ongoing programs and faculty members who have been at the school for many years, they have significant responsibility for the quality of instruction within the school. This discussion will focus on two important elements: what high-quality, flexible instruction looks like in the twenty-first century and methods principals can use to ensure that such instruction takes place.

High-quality instruction focuses on research-based strategies of effective teaching. Such strategies are discussed in detail in books and trade journals for teachers. Many colleges of education throughout the nation now regularly instruct students in these instructional methods. The methods look different for each grade level and with each content subject. However, all good instruction ensures that standards for student learning are clear to the students. Students will know what they are expected to do and/or know. Furthermore, all instruction will focus on bringing students from where they are to where they need to be, in accordance with the standard(s).

Flexible instruction is the next step in the discussion of high-quality teaching. Not all students will start out in the same place, and not all students will learn at the same rate—or in the same way. Teachers who are comfortable with lecturing and testing may need to be assisted as they learn new approaches so that all students will be guaranteed mastery of content. Lecturing, as many of us know, does not work for all students. The term *differentiation* describes teachers' efforts to meet various students' learning needs. For example, some students need more visual support than auditory support, others need extra time, and some need extra assistance. Differentiation helps ensure that all students reach the same standard.

In addition to designing differentiated instructional activities so that all students can meet standards, teachers need sufficient materials in which to provide instruction. Often, technology is important in the delivery of differentiated instruction. Furthermore, many students need additional out-of-class support that may be available through tutoring and pull-out services.

Principals can encourage high-quality, flexible instruction by providing the conditions it requires: (a) knowledge, (b) encouragement, and (c) support.

Knowledge is both pedagogical and content knowledge. Many teachers are not familiar with all the pedagogical (teaching) strategies available. Learning such strategies is time consuming but important. Principals can support this learning by providing high-quality professional development. With professional development funds, teachers can attend workshops and purchase trade books. Teachers also can get a better understanding of content through professional development. Both pedagogical and content knowledge can be fostered through professional learning communities. Such communities provide teachers time and space to discuss current teaching problems and generate solutions.

Principals can provide encouragement in two ways. First, teachers need to know that they can attain high standards. Schools that focus on providing teachers with a supportive, helpful climate have teachers who feel more positive about working toward difficult goals. Second, teachers need to know that they are expected to work toward higher standards. For this to occur, principals must be highly visible on campus, doing walk-throughs, attending department meetings, and staying around for entire sessions of school professional development. (When principals do not attend required professional development, teachers often view the training as unimportant.) Principals should engage teachers in discussion of their work, ask them about their lessons, and help them focus on utilizing better instructional strategies.

Finally, support comes through assistance provided by the principal, on-site coaches, and teacher-leaders. Teachers need to feel safe in making mistakes. They need to know that it is okay to experiment with new strategies. Principals especially can encourage this by sending positive signals about new classroom strategies they see teachers use.

Overall, it is critical that principals spend a considerable portion of each day on the improvement of instructional programs. They need to come across to teachers as highly concerned about providing students with the best instruction possible.

Skill 5.5   Use formative and summative student assessment data to develop, support, and improve campus instructional strategies and goals.

The evaluation of students is an important aspect of the teaching and learning process. Periodic testing assesses learning outcomes based on the objectives established for learning, and it provides information at various stages in the learning process to determine future learning needs such as periodic reviews, reteaching, and enrichment. As the end process, the evaluation of students' performance measures the level of goal attainment as a result of the learning activities planned by the teacher. At varying stages of the teaching and learning process, the intended outcome must be measured and the level of goal attainment established to proceed with this continuous cycle of student evaluation.

The Texas student standardized testing program began in 1980 with the first administration of the Texas Assessment of Basic Skills (TABS). The testing program has expanded over the years due to federal and state requirements. In spring 2012, the State of Texas Assessments of Academic Readiness (STAAR®) replaced the Texas Assessment of Knowledge and Skills (TAKS). STAAR represents the fifth generation of the testing program. Each new generation has been more rigorous than the one before it.

The STAAR program includes annual assessments for the following:

- Reading and mathematics at grades 3–8
- Writing at grades 4 and 7
- Science at grades 5 and 8
- Social studies at grade 8
- End-of-course assessments for English I, English II, Algebra I, biology, and U.S. history.

STAAR emphasizes readiness standards, which are the knowledge and skills that are considered most important for success in the grade or course subject that follows and for college and career. For students to be successful on the STAAR test, teachers must emphasize critical/inferential thinking, problem solving, and application rather than isolated skills.

The terms *evaluation* and *measurement* often are used interchangeably to imply the same process. However, while closely related, they should be differentiated. *Evaluation* is the process of making judgments regarding student performance, and *measurement* is the actual data collection that is used to make judgments of student performance. Evaluation is related to student performance when how well a student carries out a given task is measured or when a student's work or product is the focus of the measurement.

The purpose of the student evaluation will determine the type of process to use. Diagnostic, formative, and summative evaluations are the three types of student evaluations most commonly used. *Diagnostic evaluation* is provided prior to instruction to identify problems, to place students in certain groups, and to make assignments that are appropriate to their needs. While it is important to address the specific needs of students, teachers must be cautious of the ramifications of grouping children in homogeneous groups versus heterogeneous groups. It may appear time effective to group and work with children of like situations, but this can fail to foster students' intellectual and social growth and development. In fact, it has been proven that children in mixed groups benefit from the diversity within the group.

Formative evaluation is used to obtain feedback during the instructional process. It informs teachers of the extent to which students are learning the concepts and skills being taught. The information obtained through the formative process should lead to modification in the teaching and learning process to address specific needs of the students before reaching the end of the unit. Formative evaluation is designed to promote learning. Therefore, it must be done frequently using the specific objectives stated for learning outcomes. *Summative evaluation* is used to culminate a unit or series of lessons to arrive at a grade. It is the sum of the accomplishments of the student over a specified period of learning. Knowing the content studied and having the specific skills required to score well on tests are two different endeavors, which require not only learning content but also following form.

Often, standardized tests are considered to be summative evaluations. Therefore, it is the responsibility of teachers to train the students in test-taking skills like following directions, managing time effectively, and giving special attention to the type of tests and the skills required.

Regardless of the type of assessment, educators must gather and analyze the information it yields to determine problem areas. The teacher should discuss the problem areas with the students collectively and individually and also present them as items for discussion at teacher conferences with parents. Whether diagnostic, formative, or summative, the evaluation of student performance should be a continuous process.

The accuracy of student evaluation is essential. Accuracy is related to consistency of measurement, which is observed through reliability and validity of the instruments used to measure student performance and the usability of the instrument.

Validity is the extent to which a test measures what it is intended to measure. For example, a test may lack validity if it was designed to measure the creative writing of students but is used to measure handwriting.

Reliability refers to the consistency of the test to measure what it should measure. For example, the items on a true or false quiz, given by a classroom teacher, are reliable if they convey the same meaning every time the quiz is administered to similar groups of students under similar situations. In other words, there is no ambiguity or confusion with the items on the quiz.

Usability refers to practical considerations such as scoring procedures, level of difficulty, and time to administer the test. The usability of a test will be questionable if the scoring procedures had to be changed to accommodate local financial circumstances or if the allotted time for the test had to be reduced because of other circumstances.

Because the purpose of assessment instruments is gathering data, it is important to use various information-gathering tools to assess the knowledge and progress of students. Standardized achievement tests have become a central component of education today, particularly due to No Child Left Behind. The widespread use of standardized achievement tests to provide information for accountability to the public has driven many teachers to teach to the test and embrace more objective formats of teaching and learning. Although these tests are limited in what they measure, too often they are used to make major decisions for which they are not designed.

Standardized achievement measurements can be **norm-referenced** or **criterion-referenced**. In *norm-referenced* measurements, the performance of the student is compared with the performance of other students who took the same test. The original group of students who took the test establishes the norm. Norms can be based on age, sex, grade level, geographical location, ethnicity, or other broad classifications. Standardized norm-referenced achievement tests are designed to measure what a student knows in a particular subject in relation to other students who have similar characteristics. The test batteries provide a broad scope of content-area coverage so that they may be used on a large scale in many different states and school districts. They do not measure the goals and content emphasized in a particular local curriculum. Therefore, using standardized tests to assess the success of the curriculum or teachers' effectiveness should be avoided (McMillan, 1997).

Norm-referenced standardized achievement tests produce scores that are useful in different ways. The most common types of scores are the percentile rank or percentile score, grade equivalent score, stanine, and percentage of items answered correctly. The percentile score indicates how a student's performance compares to the norming group. It shows the percentage of the norming group that was outscored by a particular student taking the test. The scores are indicative of relative strengths and weaknesses. A student may show consistent strength in language arts and consistent weakness in mathematics. Yet one could not base remediation solely on these conclusions without a closer item analysis or a closer review of the objectives measured by the test.

The grade equivalent score is expressed by year and month in school for each student. It is used to measure growth and progress. It indicates where a student stands in reference to the norming group.

The stanine score indicates where the score is located on the normal curve for the norming group. Stanines are statistically determined, but they are not as precise as percentile ranking because they give only the area in which the score is located, not the precise location. Using stanines to report standard scores is practical and easy to understand for many parents and school personnel. Stanines range from one to nine (1–9), with five being the middle of the distribution.

Finally, achievement test scores can be reported by percentage of items answered correctly. This form of reporting may not be very meaningful when there are few items in a particular area. This makes it difficult to determine if the student guessed correctly or chose the correct responses.

Criterion-referenced standardized achievement tests are designed to measure student performance that is directly related to specific educational objectives, thus indicating what the student can or cannot do. For example, the test may measure how well a student can subtract by regrouping in the tens place or how well a student can identify the long vowel sound in specific words. Criterion-referenced tests are specific to a particular curriculum, which allows the determination of the effectiveness of the curriculum and the specific skills acquired by the students. They also provide information needed to plan for future student needs. The test scores are reported by percentage of items answered correctly to indicate mastery or non-mastery. The STAAR test is a criterion-referenced test.

Aptitude tests are another type of standardized test that measure the cognitive ability of students. They also measure potential and capacity for learning. Although they do not test specific academic ability, the ability level is influenced by the child's experiences in and out of the academic setting. Aptitude tests are used to predict achievement and determine advanced placement of students.

Teacher-made tests are evaluative instruments designed by classroom teachers to measure the attainment of objectives. Although they lack scientific validity, they serve the immediate purpose of measuring instructional outcomes. Teacher-made tests should be constructed to measure specific objectives, but they also should take into account the nature of the behavior that is being measured. Among teacher-made test question types are multiple choice, essay, matching, alternative choices (yes/no, true/false), and completion (fill in the blanks).

Portfolio assessment is fast becoming a leading form of teacher assessment. For this type of assessment, the student and teacher collect sample work in a systematic and organized manner to provide evidence of accomplishments and progress toward specific objectives.

Certainly, testing is important in the assessment of students' progress, but there are other sources of information that can be used for assessment. For example, conferencing can provide factual information for effective assessment, and a student's cumulative records also may provide factual information for cognitive and psychomotor assessments. Other information sources include interviews, diaries, self-assessment, observation, simulations, and other creative forms.

Skill 5.6   Facilitate the use and integration of technology, telecommunications, and information systems to enhance learning.

The rapid proliferation of technology has had profound effects on the evolution of teaching and learning. However, teachers report that simply keeping up with new instructional technologies, let alone integrating them productively into their teaching, can be a significant challenge (Sorcinelli, Austin, Eddy, and Beach, 2006; Zhu, Kaplan, and Dershimer, 2011).

The introduction of technology in a learning environment should not be based on technology for technology's sake, but rather on a calculated and planned agenda in which technology will be used to address identified needs.

The classroom environment, in many instances, is characterized by teachers being at the center of attention, performing, and students acting as passive vessels, consuming knowledge and information. A learning environment characterized by technology, however, offers a much different scene, and a different model of teaching and learning unfolds. It is a student-centered, constructivist model, in which students are challenged to engage in higher-order thinking skills, interact with technology at their own level, and learn what interests them.

Technology provides numerous tools that teachers can use in and out of the classroom to enhance student learning. However, keep in mind that any tool's learning benefits are contingent upon how, where, when, and why you use it.

Blackboard

The Blackboard Learning Management System (LMS) is a virtual learning environment that enhances teaching and learning by providing content management and sharing, online assessments, student tracking, assignment management, and virtual collaboration. Its main purposes are to add online elements to courses traditionally delivered face-to-face and to develop completely online courses with few or no face-to-face meetings.

Canvas

Canvas is an open source LMS by Instructure that allows teachers to collaboratively design and/or transfer their curriculum to a professional e-learning environment where students can access it anytime, anyplace, and on any device. In February 2012, Canvas K-12 was launched, an LMS platform designed for the specific needs of elementary and secondary schools.[14] The LMS enrolls parents with their students to provide greater visibility into their children's learning experience and provides actionable analytics to teachers and administrators.

Presentation Software

Sometimes it's helpful to provide visual aids to complement teaching, stimulate discussion, or allow out-of-class review. Tools designed for this purpose, such as PowerPoint or Prezi, can be effective when used thoughtfully.

Classroom Response Systems ("Clickers")

One way to encourage student engagement is by using electronic devices that allow students to record their answers to multiple-choice questions and allow you to instantly display the results. The anonymity encourages participation, and students' answers help the teacher know when further discussion is needed. Clickers also can serve as a catalyst for discussion.

Online Projects and Collaboration Tools (OCTs)

Students demonstrate significantly greater learning gains in terms of recall of basic knowledge and critical thinking when collaborating than when working independently. Technology can support student collaboration for creating new knowledge, reflecting on what they are learning, or working together to achieve a deeper understanding of course material. "The cloud," Google Docs, wikis, and blogs are examples of OCTs that have been used to enhance student learning.

Information Visualization Tools

Technology also can clarify and stimulate thought by transforming words into pictures. By creating infographics and by using tools such as Google maps, concept mapping, and Piktochart, students think more critically by visually structuring information.

Flipping the Classroom

Sometimes a great way to move students toward higher levels of understanding is to move the lecture out of the classroom and use in-person time for interactions that require applying, synthesizing, and creating. "Flipping" doesn't have to use technology, but tools such as videos, podcasts, online quizzes, and the like can help coordinate in-class and out-of-class activity.

Podcasts
Whether teachers want students to listen to information before they come to class or make an audio recording available to them for review, there are many reasons to create podcasts.

Games
What could be more engaging than a good game used well? Whether using the format of *Jeopardy* or *Who Wants to Be a Millionaire*, using games to teach, review, or personalize learning can be motivating and engaging for students.

Principals can and should use all the tools mentioned above as they communicate with teaching staff and campus stakeholders. Use of technology can enhance communication and engagement in all levels of school management.

Technology in Efficient School Operations
In addition to improving teaching and learning, technology can improve the efficiency of school operations. A principal must have the ability to make policy and decisions governing the use of technological resources. A principal also must have knowledge of computer terminology and its instructional and administrative applications and an understanding of the impact of technology in the school environment.

The principal must plan for all aspects of integrating technology in a school. Determining hardware and software requirements is essential in the process. Identifying goals and objectives for the use of technology is also important. To ensure that technology implementation proceeds unhindered, policy statements and procedures governing technology must be in place. Will the introduction of technology address productivity, administrative functions, or student achievement? In each of the situations, a different set of resources, policies, and decisions regarding the implementation will need to be established. A principal needs to understand salient issues in each area to make informed decisions.

Skill 5.7   Facilitate the implementation of sound, research-based theories and techniques of teaching, learning, classroom management, student discipline, and school safety to ensure a campus environment conducive to teaching and learning.

The dynamics of classroom management generally correspond to the leadership styles of individual teachers. An autocratic leadership style yields a punitive, harsh, and critical classroom environment. A laissez-faire leadership style, in contrast, yields a permissive classroom environment where disorder and anarchy dominate. The democratic leadership style is characteristic of today's school reform, which expects a participatory classroom. The democratic leadership style yields a classroom that is firm but friendly, encouraging and stimulating, caring and guiding. Most importantly, fairness prevails as a way of resolving conflicts (Moore, 1995).

Regardless of the discipline model endorsed by the school, the effectively managed classroom follows basic principles generated by research. Discipline models such as PBIS (Positive Behavior Intervention and Supports), the Glasser Model, the Lee Canter Assertive Discipline Model, and others dealing with prevention and correction of misbehavior may produce good results based on the teacher's leadership/management style and philosophy. Yet, a general focus on procedures to manage and prevent behavioral problems may prove more effective than many of the leading models. Current educational research supports structure, such as beginning class on time, setting up classroom procedures and routines, and keeping desk and storage spaces clean and organized from the beginning of the school year.

Making a smooth and orderly transition between activities cuts down on the idle time that generally encourages misbehavior. Making eye contact with students, being respectful of them, and reinforcing positive interaction with and among them provide a healthy learning atmosphere. Having a general sense of what is going on in the classroom at all times, giving verbal and nonverbal encouragement, and stopping misbehavior in a firm and consistent manner as soon as it occurs, without using threats, conveys constancy of purpose and expectations. Careful instructional planning and pace of teaching also reduce opportunities for problems. Additionally, involving the parents as partners prevents discipline problems and provides a support for solutions to problems as they occur.

Skill 5.8 Facilitate the development, implementation, evaluation, and refinement of student services and activity programs to fulfill academic, developmental, social, and cultural needs.

The role of the principal has changed significantly in the past ten years. Prior to this, principals were the managers of the school building: they made sure all aspects were working together according to specification. They ensured that activities were safe and cost effective, that students were behaving properly, and that teachers had the resources they needed.

Lately, there has been a shift to considering principals as instructional leaders. They are expected to be thoroughly aware of each classroom, the instructional styles of each teacher, and the learning outcomes of all students. In summary, they are held responsible for the quality of instruction and the depth of learning at their schools.

With this shift of responsibilities comes a dilemma for most school leaders: Should they focus on instruction at the expense of other areas they know to be effective for student growth and development of a positive school culture? Or do they try to balance both demands—which takes much more time, money, and effort?

Most principals would argue that both demands are necessary, no matter the cost. They realize that students, their families, and teachers need to see that all students' needs are met on a variety of levels. Schools are ideal places to provide athletic, creative, and intellectual activities. Furthermore, these activities provide schools with a greater sense of community.

First, principals must focus on the school's mission. Most schools think beyond test scores and student achievement in their mission statements. For example, a school that says that its mission is to prepare students to succeed in a changing world must acknowledge that achievement is important. However, such a school also will offer students opportunities to succeed socially, physically, and creatively. As school needs are identified to reach those broad goals, principals can select faculty to participate and set aside money. As they allocate school resources—money, personnel, time, and space—they must ensure that students are treated fairly and equally. For example, directing significant resources to the football team—and few resources to the chess team—likely will be seen as unfair.

In addition to activities, principals must ensure that unpredictable student services needs are met. For example, a highly bureaucratic student services office may not respond quickly when emergencies arise and students need counseling en masse. Such offices also need to pay close attention to the requests of parents. Principals can help ensure this by instituting planning sessions and regular meetings to review policies, procedures, and school goals. Student services office staff should play critical roles throughout the campus so that they see the concerns and needs of teachers, as well as students, when they are in academic and athletic environments.

Skill 5.9 Analyze instructional needs and allocate resources effectively and equitably.

Many principals do not have control over entire personnel budgets (usually, district human resource offices control personnel issues at school sites), but schools often have discretion over many resources, including materials, additional funding, and support services. In an age of accountability, funding for student achievement must also be in place. For a principal to make sense of the instructional needs at a school, various analyses must be done. First, by looking at student achievement, principals can see which groups of students require more resources. When referring to resources, the term *equity* is often used. This term may imply that all students should get the same resources—or the same level of monetary allocations. However, the current thinking is that to reach certain standards, different students will require different resources. Therefore, when leaders think about allocating resources effectively and equitably, it is helpful to consider the term *adequacy*. In other words, leaders can ask this question: What is adequate in providing each student what he or she needs to reach standards at high levels?

Another way to analyze instructional needs is to examine how money is allocated to various parts of a campus and to determine which areas need a reallocation of funds to support student achievement. When doing this, principals face great scrutiny from stakeholders who are negatively affected by shifts in allocations. Principals are more successful in this work when they enlist the support of a variety of stakeholders.

Finally, it is critical that principals make their practices public—to faculty, to parents, to the district, and to the community. Small monetary issues are outside the interest of most stakeholders; however, the information should be available— and even discussed—because school funds are derived from taxpayers. Furthermore, when monetary decisions are public, support for decisions is acquired more easily.

Skill 5.10   Analyze the implications of various factors (e.g., staffing patterns, class scheduling formats, school organizational structures, student discipline practices) for teaching and learning.

Many factors influence teaching and learning in schools. Often, it is hard for teachers to see the impact of various factors because they are most familiar with what happens in their own classrooms once they close their doors. Yet, the entire structure of the school and school day sends many messages about values. The following paragraphs examine a variety of factors separately.

Staffing Patterns
Who is teaching the students makes a significant difference in how students learn. Regulations limit how teachers are hired and fired, so many principals must learn to coexist with teachers who may not be very good. However, principals can find ways of minimizing the impact of poor teachers on the neediest students. Additionally, some teachers have specific strengths, and other teachers have entirely different strengths. It is useful to ensure that teachers are assigned so that students benefit from as many teachers' strengths as possible.

Class Schedule Formats
Particularly at the secondary level, schedule formats are critical to successful student learning. Many schools now see the value of block scheduling, a format that allows classes to meet for much longer periods of time on an alternating day schedule. Other schools have combined social studies with language arts or

math with science to encourage cross-disciplinary studies. Some schools have students clustered in "houses," where all teachers rotate the same group of students. The purpose of this format is to allow teachers to discuss specific student issues. At the elementary level, class scheduling might permit students to be grouped homogeneously for specific subjects. This allows teachers in those subjects to work more closely with specific student issues. At other times, students can be grouped heterogeneously to provide a diverse climate among students.

School Organizational Structures

In secondary schools, organizational structures typically are departments or grade-level configurations. In elementary schools, organizational structure is based on grade levels and non-core subjects. In both cases, organizational structures have a bearing on scheduling, physical location, and personnel. For example, secondary schools that have "houses" typically are better positioned to deal with students' emotional issues. A student's teachers would have better access to one another—in a physical sense—to provide services and support. At the elementary level, an organizational structure that allows grade-level teachers to work in physical proximity to special needs teachers is conducive to better collaboration on students learning requirements.

Student Discipline Practices

From a student motivation perspective—as well as a building climate perspective—the ways in which a school handles discipline directly impact teaching and learning. High expectations with reasonable consequences must be clear to all students and teachers. Fair procedures must be followed. Teachers need to know that if they send students out of their classrooms, then they must follow procedures. The attitude at a school is more productive when the emphasis is taken off of rules and consequences and instead put on fairness, kindness, and other positive elements. When everyone sees that the school values equity more than it values rule-following, people in the school will be more inclined to consider the value of the rules.

Skill 5.11   Ensure responsiveness to diverse sociological, linguistic, cultural, and other factors that may affect students' development and learning.

Schools are complex social systems, involving a diverse range of students and teachers. Principals have success at running schools when they can find ways to ensure that all students' sociological, linguistic, and cultural concerns are attended to. The following paragraphs discuss each of these issues in more depth.

Sociological issues are important because schools deal directly with children, who at different stages of development undergo significant emotional and physical changes. As we have seen with shootings, gang activity, and other tragedies that have occurred at schools, many issues are important besides student achievement. Schools must be places where students feel safe, accepted, and valued. Particularly during some of the more challenging phases of student development, such as adolescence, schools must focus on ensuring that bullying does not take place. When principals reiterate messages to schools about the importance of keeping the campus safe, secure, and welcoming for all students, all stakeholders get the message that mean, discriminative, dangerous, and illegal activities are not tolerated under any circumstances.

Linguistic issues are critical in a population that is increasingly diverse. Students come from many cultures and often speak different languages at home. While bilingual and English Language Learner programs deal directly with the academic issues of second language learners, the school culture also must be positioned to deal with such issues. Students in schools where bilingual support is provided must understand that second language learners are valued, both in the classroom and when participating in school activities, governance, and athletics. Excluding ELL students from any part of school life does a huge disservice to these students, to the detriment of the whole school culture. Principals must make sure that all second language learners feel like they are part of the whole school at all times.

Finally, cultural issues are important in multiple ways. Teachers must be sensitive to students' cultural biases and assumptions in the classroom. Culturally relevant instruction is a concept that has become important to public schooling over the last few years. It suggests that because students come from different cultures, they will learn things in different ways. Teachers, therefore, must be attentive to students' background knowledge, culture, religion, sexual orientation, and so on. Even if some information is not known, teachers need to be aware that all students will see information in different ways. While a final standard for each academic area must be met, there are many ways for students to learn that information. Principals can model that behavior with teachers and continually encourage teachers and students to consider thoughts from others' perspectives.

COMPETENCY 6.0   **THE PRINCIPAL KNOWS HOW TO IMPLEMENT A STAFF EVALUATION AND DEVELOPMENT SYSTEM TO IMPROVE THE PERFORMANCE OF ALL STAFF MEMBERS, SELECT AND IMPLEMENT APPROPRIATE MODELS FOR SUPERVISION AND STAFF DEVELOPMENT, AND APPLY THE LEGAL REQUIREMENTS FOR PERSONNEL MANAGEMENT.**

Skill 6.1   **Work collaboratively with other campus personnel to develop, implement, evaluate, and revise a comprehensive campus professional development plan that addresses staff needs and aligns professional development with identified goals.**

Career and staff development refers to the continual process of increasing the skills of professionals within the organization. The methods of staff development are numerous; however, the evidence of impact of most methods is sparse. It is important to understand what works and what doesn't work when finding new ways to improve the skills of school staff members.

Let us first differentiate between career development and staff development. Career development is deliberate training and practice meant to move a person into another career stage. For example, teachers who feel the call to school leadership typically go back to school and earn a master's degree and principal certification. Usually, this process takes place outside the schooling organization (at universities), although some districts are experimenting with in-house training programs.

Staff development, typically the domain of school districts, is meant to increase the skills of people currently in positions. So, while teachers may have been trained as teachers in certification programs, they will constantly need to be taught new strategies, skills, and techniques to use in their classrooms. Furthermore, good staff development helps motivate teachers to improve their practice further.

The old model of staff development consisted of teaching discrete skills to teachers, often in impersonal large groups. Staff development topics have often been irrelevant to most teachers, and they typically included no follow-up for teachers to discuss or reflect on new learning. Even though this is considered the "old" model of staff development, these methods persist in many schools and districts across the country. Gradually, schools and districts are learning that this model does not improve teacher practice and student learning.

The new model of staff development focuses on specific skills tailored to specific teacher needs. It includes significant follow-up time, sustained learning, and collaborative discussion. This model is specific in that it typically deals with individual subject areas or teacher techniques related to a particular grade level or subject. For example, instead of teaching all teachers in a high school about a particular technique, teachers in each department would learn things related to what they typically teach.

Additionally, the new model of staff development focuses on sustaining learning. Instead of providing teachers with a single training session, the new model of staff development encourages continual study of a topic throughout a school year. For example, teachers might learn a new strategy at the beginning of the year so that they can try it out for a few months. Then, possibly halfway through the year, the topic can be brought up again in a staff development session so that teachers can learn new strategies to deal with some of the problems they have experienced with it in their "trial" period. Later in the year, teachers can get together to further reflect on the strategy and plan how they will use it in upcoming years.

Skill 6.2 Facilitate the application of adult learning principles and motivation theory to all campus professional development activities, including the use of appropriate content, processes, and contexts.

Baron (1992) defines *motivation* as a force that energizes, sustains, and channels behavior toward a goal. Theorists maintain that there are two types of motivation. One is intrinsic motivation, which results from an individual's internal drive state and provides impetus toward goal attainment. The other is extrinsic motivation, which uses external incentives and rewards to motivate goal achievement. Providing for the needs, desires, and preferences of individuals in an organizational setting influences motivation and influences the objectives of the organization. Motivating individuals is a complex process of trying to facilitate desired motivational patterns (Hoy and Miskel, 1996). A number of theories have been developed to explain what influences individuals to work enthusiastically, to want to engage in professional growth, to contribute to goal attainment in organizations, and to act responsibly.

Organizations have goals and objectives they seek to achieve. These goals and objectives depend on people facilitating them. The question of how to get people motivated to achieve those goals and objectives, expeditiously and effectively, is at the heart of motivational theories. Theories of motivation are grouped into the categories of *behavioral, cognitive*, and *humanistic.* The behavioral approach to motivation suggests that motivation depends upon the effectiveness of reinforcers. Using specific reinforcers to influence behavior is an important element in the behavioral approach.

Cognitive theory suggests that there are two personal factors to consider in relation to motivation—expectations and beliefs (Eggen and Kauchak, 1997). When there is the expectation that one can succeed at a task, and value to achieving that task is attached, then a feeling of self-efficacy emerges. In an organization, leaders may ask what can be done to increase a sense of self-efficacy in the organization's members.

The humanistic perspective views motivation as people's attempts to reach their potential (Eggen and Kauchak, 1997). Motivation proceeds from internal mechanisms that cause individuals to achieve, grow and develop, and reach their potential.

An organization can use incentives and rewards to motivate individuals to be more productive. The environmental factors that tend to make the workplace enjoyable or distasteful are important in any work environment. Principals' attention to these factors, which will permeate the workplace and, subsequently, have an impact on the motivation of organizations' members to accomplish tasks, have a bearing on the fulfillment of organizational goals. Because individuals have needs, desires, likes, and dislikes that are related to their motivation, the principal must understand these and how they relate to work.

Currently, educational policy relies on the idea of external motivation to improve instructional quality. No Child Left Behind operates largely on the principle that rewards and punishments will increase motivation levels of teachers, principals, and students. While growth targets are incremental, when they are not met, schools and staff may, for example, be transferred to other schools in the district. It is uncertain how effective external motivation is for improving the learning of all students across the country.

Skill 6.3 Allocate appropriate time, funding, and other needed resources to ensure the effective implementation of professional development plans.

Professional development is a crucial component of successful school change. New standards and accountability systems demand more of teachers than ever before, and many teachers simply do not have the skills or knowledge to implement the many things for which they are responsible.

Significant research on professional development has concluded that among the worst ways of helping teachers learn new skills or knowledge is by putting them through a "one-shot" staff in-service. A staff in-service is a session that focuses on a particular strategy or technique for the classroom. Sometimes, these sessions are one to two hours. Other times, they are five to six hours. In either case, these sessions give teachers no reason to apply their new learning and do not take into account adult learning theory, which suggests that adults learn best when they have an immediate application for their learning. Since most staff development sessions have no follow-up (for example, discussion about how the strategy worked or one-on-one coaching), most teachers don't try the new strategies because they feel safe and comfortable with their current strategies.

Effective professional development consists of deep learning across time with significant opportunities for follow-up, discussion, assistance, and reflection. Often, when professional development sessions on a topic are spread out over a whole year (for example, one three-hour session per month), teachers have more reason to follow through and try new ideas in the classroom. When schools add components of professional learning communities—group configurations that allow for discussion of new learning—then teachers have more opportunity to reflect, discuss, and question the new ideas. This allows teachers to work through personal concerns and problems they might be facing in their classrooms.

Consistently, teachers report in surveys that they never have enough time to learn new strategies. Therefore, it is crucial that professional development not be limited to a few hours per year. Schools must provide teachers with multiple opportunities, often by rearranging the school day, so that teachers can interact with one another and with new teaching ideas on a more regular basis.

Funds for professional development also are critical. While grants are often available, principals must be creative about providing teachers with the resources they need to be effective. If teachers do not get these professional development resources, it directly impacts student learning. Therefore, principals must view allocation for professional development as a necessity—not as a financial burden.

Skill 6.4   Implement effective, appropriate, and legal strategies for the recruitment, screening, selection, assignment, induction, development, evaluation, promotion, discipline, and dismissal of campus staff.

Educational leaders in schools must possess a number of competencies. The most time-consuming competency involves human resource management and development. Educational leaders must know and understand human relations because labor accounts for 80% to 90% of a school's budget. Personnel management roles for principals have expanded over the years. An understanding of the aspects and importance of personnel management in achieving the vision and mission of schools is essential in creating and maintaining a successful and efficient school organization.

The principal must lead the staff in a collegial environment to achieve the mission of the school. To do this, the principal must possess an attitude that people are of greatest importance in organizations, particularly in schools. When the principal provides satisfying, useful work for the instructional and noninstructional personnel, they are empowered to do what is best for the students.

In selecting instructional personnel, the principal has many responsibilities. Planning, recruitment, and selection are essential aspects of securing personnel.

Planning requires the principal to look at the current staff and plan for short-term and long-term personnel needs. Planning should occur within the context of site-based management. The principal involves the school personnel in developing and revising the personnel plan for the school. All other aspects of the school's program have to be considered in this process. Thus, personnel are evaluated in terms of the current strengths and needs of the staff, students, parents, community, school district, state laws and rules, and federal rules and regulations. Facilities, equipment, and other factors also must be reviewed at this time. Planning must be comprehensive and must take place well in advance of the need. The plan must allow sufficient time for the principal to prepare papers and get approval through the district system. The principal must know the process used in the school district to select personnel, including how assignments are determined. The plan also must provide for emergencies such as unexpected promotions, illnesses, resignations, and terminations.

Once the plan is completed, recruitment is the next step in obtaining personnel. Recruitment is critical to successful human resource management. Only persons in the applicant pool may be considered for employment. Thus, it is important to recruit sufficient numbers of qualified persons to meet the school's needs. The most important factor should be the quality of the applicants. Each district has its own procedure for recruiting personnel. If the district does the recruiting, the principal has to inform the district early and get approval to fill the positions. The principal who has to recruit the staff must make contacts early. The principal must contact college and university career offices and schools of education that promise the greatest possibility of supplying the kinds of personnel needed. Career fairs on college and university campuses at the state and local levels are another means of recruiting personnel. Dialogue with colleagues and current school staff offer other opportunities to recruit new employees. Recruitment activities can be tailored to increase the diversity of the school's staff. The process of obtaining staff is best handled through a selection committee.

The selection process involves screening the paperwork, interviewing candidates and checking references. Using the job-related criteria for each position, the selection process requires that each applicant's papers are evaluated against the criteria. Applicants whose qualifications do not meet these criteria are removed from the pool of applicants. The quality of the application is also judged for such factors as neatness, comprehensiveness, job stability, competencies, English errors, and training. Field of certification is a crucial factor to consider in selecting staff members. These files are confidential and should be used only by trained teachers, parents, students, and others who serve on the selection committee.

Applicants who meet the training and experience qualifications for the position are reviewed, and a determination is made to interview. The interview is the most time-consuming step in the process of selecting personnel. The selection committee determines and notifies each applicant of the time and location for the interview. Prior to the interview, the committee must determine questions and criteria to judge responses. All candidates for a position must be asked the same questions and judged by the same criteria. The selection committee submits the names of the most qualified applicants, usually three to five persons, listed alphabetically, to the principal.

The principal reviews the work of the committee, interviews the potential employees, and does a reference check. Persons on and not on the reference list should be contacted. Visiting the applicant's place of employment is another good strategy to use. Principals often contact applicants at the institutions that trained them to get professional judgments about the candidate. Fingerprint records should be checked to ensure that known criminals are not employed. The principal recommends to the superintendent the person who should be employed.

Finally, with No Child Left Behind and its emphasis on "highly qualified teachers," principals will have to abide by state and federal laws regarding certification levels and degrees. *All teachers teaching core subject academic areas are required to meet specific competency and educational requirements.* For example, all secondary subject-area teachers must have a degree (or demonstrate extensive competency, usually through a very rigorous exam) in the subjects they will be teaching.

Newly hired employees receive assistance through the induction process. The induction process ranges from 90 days to a full school year. The best induction approach is one in which the teachers are assisted throughout the year by a mentor teacher who teaches the same grade level and subjects. The induction process should be based upon the orientation and should extend the orientation to cover every aspect of the work for the position. Beginning teachers need more assistance than experienced teachers. The first part of the induction process is orientation. Teachers new to a school must be oriented to the procedures, paper requirements, teaching and learning expectations, rules, and all aspects of the school culture. In some districts, the district does the orientation, with the school providing additional orientation for those factors unique to that school. The socialization process is critical because it can determine whether personnel become or fail to become contributing members of the teaching/learning community.

The Professional Development and Appraisal System (PDAS) remains in place as the State's approved instrument for appraising its teachers and identifying areas that would benefit from staff development. Cornerstones of the process include a minimum of one 45-minute observation and completion of the Teacher Self-Report form.

PDAS includes 51 criteria within eight domains reflecting the Proficiencies for Learner-Centered Instruction adopted in 1997 by the State Board for Educator Certification (SBEC). The domains are as follows:

1 Active, Successful Student Participation in the Learning Process
2 Learner-centered Instruction
3 Evaluation and feedback on Student Progress
4 Management of Student Discipline, Instructional Strategies, Time/Materials
5 Professional Communication
6 Professional Development
7 Compliance with Policies, Operating Procedures and Requirements

It takes careful documentation and an understanding of due process law to remove a teacher who is detrimental to the well-being of the school. Dismissing a tenured teacher should never be taken lightly. However, the failure to act in the face of teacher incompetence compromises the morale of the school and the education of its students.

In Texas, a teacher whose performance meets any of the following circumstances will be designated as a "teacher in need of assistance":

1. A teacher who is evaluated as unsatisfactory in one or more Professional Development and Appraisal System (PDAS) domains
2. A teacher who is evaluated as below expectations in two or more domains

An intervention plan may be developed at any time at the discretion of the appraiser when the appraiser has documentation that would potentially produce an evaluation rating of "below expectations" or "unsatisfactory."

When a teacher is designated as a teacher in need of assistance, the appraiser and/or the teacher's supervisor shall, in consultation with the teacher, develop an intervention plan that includes the following:

- PDAS Domain(s) in which the teacher is in need of assistance
  Example: Domain 1. Active, successful Student Participation in the Learning
- Professional improvement activities and dates for completion
- Evidence that will be used to determine that professional improvement activities have been completed
- Directives for changes in teacher behavior and timelines
- Evidence that will be used to determine if teacher behavior has changed

A compensation and reward system is required in any organization. A compensation program is directed at attracting and maintaining quality employees, motivating employees, creating incentives for continual growth, and maintaining budgetary control in school districts (Webb, Greer, Montello, and

Norton, 1996). The district must have a compensation policy. Merit pay, paid leave, child care, cost of living increases, salary schedules, extracurricular stipends, early retirement plans, tax-sheltered annuity, and medical plans are types of compensation and rewards. Retirement plans, severance pay, sick leave, annual leave, sabbatical leave, religious leave, military leave, professional leave, and transportation allowance are among the many types of compensations and rewards available to school personnel. Supply and demand often determine the extent of the package available to employees.

Many districts currently are experimenting with pay for performance plans, in which teachers who are more adept at increasing test scores are given bonuses. This has been highly controversial, though, as statistical models to determine teacher impact on student test scores is complicated and imprecise.

Skill 6.5   Use formative and summative evaluation procedures to enhance the knowledge and skills of campus staff.

Personnel appraisal is a significant responsibility of the principal. When appraisal is done correctly, teachers grow professionally and students benefit from increasingly effective instruction. Most school districts use district-wide criteria to judge teacher effectiveness. These objective measures should be published and discussed early in the year. Teachers should set professional development goals based on weak areas and should receive recognition for areas of strength.

The principal must know those responsibilities at the building level and those at the district level. The principal evaluates building-level staff, so he or she must know the criteria and how to apply each. With the advent of performance-based appraisal in Texas, principals need training to tie performance to student learning.

The processes for gathering the data used to rate teachers on the district criteria should also be published and discussed. Gossip, unsigned notes, and other such sources are unreliable and should not be used. Most often, there are formal, planned classroom observations in addition to walk-throughs and other informal methods for viewing a teacher's work. Teacher performance ratings should be tied directly to student achievement, so student achievement data should be part of what is used in determining appraisal scores. Teaching hasn't happened unless students have learned!

Teachers should be given clear feedback about whether their performance is adequately satisfying the criteria of the appraisal instrument. Delivering this feedback to the teacher in a face-to-face conference allows the appraiser to establish a dialogue with the teacher about instructional practices. Very few people change because someone talks to them. To change behavior, the thinking behind the behavior must change, prompted by asking questions that cause teachers to reflect on their own practices.

A principal's goal is to improve the staff so that student achievement will be optimized. Underperforming teachers need assistance, and they should agree with two or three improvement goals and concentrate on making progress in these areas before moving on to other areas of need. Document the improvement plan and progress, or lack of progress, toward the selected goals. Poorly trained teachers need to observe excellent models, so allow release time for observations in other classrooms. Conferencing with them after the observation will help them apply what they observed in their own classroom. When a teacher is working through an improvement plan, the principal should make more frequent visits to that teacher's classroom and look for signs of improvement. Document every visit and intervention. Ineffective teachers can improve with a principal's support, training, and mentoring.

The appraisal process also is a way to provide recognition for outstanding teachers. When a teacher's performance is highly rated, this provides encouragement to continue instructional practices that benefit students. Appraisal systems allow the structured feedback that teachers need to improve instruction and grow professionally.

Skill 6.6 Diagnose campus organizational health and morale and implement strategies to provide ongoing support to campus staff.

No Child Left Behind and statewide initiatives have created challenges to maintaining a positive school climate. Positive school climate has been recognized as the foundation of successful schools and a strong predictor of the academic success of students (Van Horn, 2003). Research has strongly supported the fact that the leadership of a school principal directly impacts the climate of the school and, in turn, the achievement of its students. The demands of today's standards-based curriculum movement and high-stakes testing are taxing administrators, students, and teachers. Aspects of today's education reform that are harming school climates include: competition between teachers and schools that reduces collegiality; rigid, scripted curriculum materials that deskill teachers and diminish creativity; and misapplication and overanalysis of test scores. For example, many elementary schools across the country have eliminated recess to increase instructional time.

The pressure has fallen squarely on the shoulders of the principals, who have to manage and mediate the full range of these demands. For example, teachers today often feel demeaned by scripted curriculum and the emphasis on test preparation and results. It is up to the principal to support the teachers in their work and help maintain equilibrium between standards-based instruction and curricular innovation, creativity, and independence. At the same time, the principal must satisfy the demands of the district administration and parents.

To improve organizational health, the principal must assess it. There are several measures of school climate, beginning with Halpin and Croft's Organizational Climate Description Questionnaire that was developed at Ohio State University. This 42-item instrument depicts schools as Open, Engaged, Disengaged, or Closed. These classifications are derived from the relationship between the two measured components of **principal behavior** and **teacher behavior**.

Principal behavior has three dimensions: directive, supportive, and restrictive. Directive behavior is when a principal acts with single-handed authority in matters that could be collaborative, such as curriculum, daily schedules, assemblies, field trips, and purchasing. A principal who jumps in to help staff in a wide range of activities, from covering classes to chaperoning school events, is supportive. Restrictive behavior is exhibited with rigidity about curriculum, behavior, and ritual.

An Open rating in principal-teacher relationships is characterized by high supportiveness, low directedness (encouraging teachers to act independently and try new ideas), and low restrictiveness (not interfering with teachers' jobs).

Teacher behavior, the second component, has three similar dimensions: engagement, intimacy, and collegiality. Engagement is a behavior that reveals a teacher with high involvement and alignment with student success and curriculum development. Intimacy describes a closeness and trust with the community, including students, staff, and families. A collegial teacher is one who shares successful curriculum and ideas and supports fellow teachers.

An Open rating in teacher-teacher behaviors is characterized by high intimacy (friendly and supportive of one another), high collegiality (accepting of, respectful of and enthusiastic toward one another) and high engagement (having interactions that are tolerant and meaningful).

The overall climate is determined by the combination of the principal behavior and teacher behavior as shown in the table below

OCDQ-RE School Climate Ratings

CLIMATE RATING	PRINCIPAL BEHAVIOR	TEACHER BEHAVIOR
Open	Open	Open
Engaged	Closed	Open
Disengaged	Open	Closed
Closed	Closed	Closed

A healthy school climate is characterized by a principal who avoids burdening teachers with bureaucratic trivia and busywork. The faculty is open to students and committed to helping them. This results in less disruptive behavior. Teachers and the principal have relationships that are open and supportive.

An Engaged climate is characterized by teachers who work together and are committed to their students, despite a principal who supervises too closely and burdens teachers with bureaucratic trivia. In this climate, the teachers work together in spite of the principal.

A Disengaged climate is the opposite of an Engaged one. In a Disengaged climate, the principal is supportive of the teachers to no avail. Faculty is indifferent to one another and may not go out of their way to help students.

A Closed climate is an unhealthy system in which distrust reigns. Teachers are often apathetic and uncaring, and the principal is often rigid and authoritarian.

Skill 6.7   Engage in ongoing professional development activities to enhance one's own knowledge and skills and to model lifelong learning.

Today's principal is recognized as a critical person for impacting instructional change and bringing to fruition the goals and objectives of a school. The kind and quality of leadership exercised by those invested with the authority to supervise school operations make a difference in the lives of students, the community, and ultimately the nation. Hence, the role of the principal and the competencies that an individual brings to this position are key to creating dynamic and effective school organizations.

Just as teachers need training to become their best, school and district-level administrators greatly benefit from professional development designed specifically for them. Principals cannot be too busy to learn. Professional development for school leaders takes many formats. Workshops (one shot or long term), seminars and conferences, mentoring, shadowing, and coaching all constitute professional development. In a Phi Delta Kappa article (March 1999), Paula Evans and Nancy Mohr suggest that teaching principals how to lead schools by giving them "predigested 'in-basket' training" rarely leads to new thinking about leadership, teaching, or learning. Reinforcing old patterns and hearing speakers who mouth familiar platitudes about the "effective" principal may make people feel comfortable, but it does not lead to substantive change.

The following are seven beliefs about how principals learn best:

- Principals' learning is personal, yet it takes place most effectively while working in groups.

- Principals foster more powerful teacher and student learning by focusing on their own learning.

- Principals must be stretched past their comfortable assumptions about ineffective practices and beliefs toward answering difficult questions that are integral to their work

- Focused reflection takes time away from "doing the work," yet it is essential.

- It takes strong leadership to have truly democratic learning.

- Rigorous planning is necessary for flexible and responsive implementation.

- New learning depends on "protected dissonance" (a safe environment in which to take risks with ideas and ask tough questions).

A unique aspect of school leadership professional development, as compared to teacher professional development frameworks, is the important element of networking and consultation. School leadership professional development must aim to create a network of collegial support in which to exchange and discuss ideas and strategies. Leadership is lonely; principals, in their positions of authority, lack such support in their individual buildings. They may be the only administrator, especially in small schools, and they may have few natural support mechanisms. If principals are to implement what they have learned and evaluate the impacts of their efforts, they will need colleagues with whom to reflect on and evaluate these outcomes.

A particularly useful tool for professional development is membership in professional organizations. In addition to providing invaluable opportunities for idea sharing and networking with other teachers and school leaders, many professional organizations publish journals that feature the latest developments in the field, assess new strategies and methodologies, and highlight new career and training opportunities.

COMPETENCY 7.0 **THE PRINCIPAL KNOWS HOW TO APPLY ORGANIZATIONAL, DECISION-MAKING, AND PROBLEM SOLVING SKILLS TO ENSURE AN EFFECTIVE LEARNING ENVIRONMENT.**

Skill 7.1 **Implement appropriate management techniques and group process skills to define roles, assign functions, delegate authority, and determine accountability for campus goal attainment.**

A principal must be in charge. The community of learners expects an ultimate source of authority. It insists that there be equity and that decisions be reached in an effective and timely manner. The principal ultimately is responsible for what happens and what does not happen in the school. Examples of being in charge include determining who does what and when in clearly stated written or oral communication, designating persons responsible for given duties, handling security measures, safeguarding the internal accounts, and ensuring safety at all school events. Recently, the principal has taken on a stronger role in instructional leadership. To be a proactive instructional leader, the principal must ensure that teachers understand expectations and are provided with the materials and training they need to be successful.

The principal accepts responsibility for what goes wrong and shares what goes right with those who made it happen. The principal understands his or her role in assuming responsibility for all required tasks and ensures that they are accomplished in a timely manner. To achieve school goals, the proactive principal will determine the barriers and ways to overcome them, avenues to achieve the goals, how best to use available human and material resources, and how to secure additional resources to achieve the goals. The reactive principal will blame others and engage in faultfinding, responding according to emotions and feelings and focusing on circumstances or people over whom they have no control.

In sum, the principal must accept the responsibility for what happens. In this process, the principal must change behavior based upon prior experiences and successes or errors. The process requires continuous evaluation and reflection on what worked or did not work and why. Through this process, the principal corrects past behavior and continues to grow and develop within a collegial environment.

Good leaders get all the facts possible on all sides of an issue prior to making a decision, unless the situation requires immediate action. At times, a leader must react to be successful. However, if the predominant leadership stance is reacting, leading will not be productive or satisfying. Today's effective principals look at their responsibilities holistically, not as a series of tasks and responses to emergencies.

To be proactive, principals must clearly delineate expectations for all stakeholders. Responses must be consistent yet fair. It is particularly important that principals "manage by walking around," a phrase used to describe a leader who is visible, knows what is going on, and does not hide in his or her office.

Delegation of Authority

Delegation is the process of sharing power and work (delivering the power from one to another). The principal cannot perform all school activities. When work is delegated, the authority to act should be provided to the subordinates, too. Delegation is a management technique used to get the things done through others, but the control remains in the hands of the superior who supervises the activities of subordinates.

Even though delegation is vital for the efficient functioning of the organization, in practice there are several factors that prevent effective delegation. These problems in delegation may be classified into three categories.

Obstacles due to superiors

Managers are often reluctant to delegate authority due to the following reasons:

- Some managers are autocratic, and they think that delegation will reduce their influence in the organization.

- Some managers think that no one can do the job as well as they can.

- An incompetent manager may not want to delegate his or her authority for fear of being exposed.

- Some managers are reluctant to accept the risk of wrong decisions that the subordinates might make. These managers lack confidence in their subordinates.

- A manager may hesitate to delegate authority if he or she has no means to ensure that his or her subordinates are using the authority properly.

Obstacles due to subordinates

The subordinates may be hesitant to accept the delegated authority due to the following reasons:

- Subordinates may be reluctant to accept delegation when they lack self-confidence.

- Some subordinates may depend excessively on their supervisor for all decisions.

- When subordinates are already overburdened with duties, they may not like additional responsibility through delegation.

- Subordinates may reject delegation of authority if no incentives are available to them.

- Subordinates may avoid delegation when adequate information, working facilities, and resources are not available.

Obstacles due to organizing weakness

Sometimes delegation may be hampered due to weakness in the organization structure. The following are some organizational weaknesses:

- Inadequate planning

- Splintered authority

- Lack of unity of command

- Absence of effective control techniques

- Lack of competent manager

- Unclear authority relationship

- Environment of internal distrust

Skill 7.2 Implement procedures for gathering, analyzing, and using data from a variety of sources for informed campus decision making.

Principals must often be forceful and feel confident about decisions made. They do not require confirmation from others, although they may discuss the situation(s) with fellow administrators, supervisors, or teachers as a means of sharing and acquiring other approaches for future use. Good leaders get all the facts possible on all sides of an issue prior to making a decision, unless it is an emergency situation that requires immediate action for the safety of people. After getting all possible facts, the principal can use best principles of management to make the correct decision and then stick with the decision unless new evidence becomes available to change the original decision. An example of this decision-making activity is for the principal to cancel a dance after an important football game because the students failed to live up to their attendance agreement for the six weeks prior to the game. The forceful principal maintains this decision despite parental and student discontent.

The old model of organizational management was predicated on a system of hierarchies. The further up on an organizational chart you were, the more information you had about the operation of the organization. The lower you were, the less information you supposedly needed to do your job effectively. If you were given a task by your superior, all you needed was enough information to complete that task.

The days of hierarchical management and limited information are long gone—at least from effective organizations. Today, effective organizations entail a large amount of information that should flow horizontally (among colleagues) and vertically (up and down the chain of command).

There are a few reasons for this. Information comes from a variety of sources, and often organizational leaders are not privileged to much of it. For example, organizational threats may be identified by those on the lowest level of the organization, and if information were not able to be communicated from the lowest level to the highest, leaders will be less effective in their efforts.

Particularly in education, innovations and effective techniques should be transferred from one employee to another. With a top-down information flow, many teachers would not receive helpful and productive information. Finally, even if some pieces of information may not directly involve someone at the lower levels of the organizational chart, the more those employees know what is going on in their organization—and the more they feel involved—the more they will be willing to invest themselves in the life of the organization. This is extremely important in schools. When teachers feel that they have more control over and understanding of the direction of the school, they will see themselves as part of a whole organization, rather than just an isolated teacher in a classroom.

Knowledge can and should be communicated in a variety of different ways. A principal communicating information to a staff of teachers should be direct, up-front, and honest. Even when it may seem that it is best to skirt around the truth or divulge only small pieces of information, being honest and direct ultimately will be more effective. Generally, in organizations such as schools, communication that is not direct and honest creates gossip or mistrust. Trust is an important facet of the operation of a school, primarily because there are so many groups of stakeholders, each with their own interests. When these groups get together, they share stories and band together to get what they want. Therefore, principals benefit themselves—as well as the whole school community—when they present information in a forthright manner. There is only one caution. Much information that principals receive is sensitive; principals should take care to divulge only appropriate information.

One way to increase the transfer of appropriate information throughout a school is through professional learning communities (PLCs). When teachers have the opportunity to discuss issues and transfer ideas, the flow of information is more effective than if information comes from a single or unofficial source.

Another good tool for information flow is technology, particularly email, websites, blogs, and other places that all stakeholders can access. Information management systems must be developed to maintain the safety of information, yet be open enough to allow access to those who need it.

Skill 7.3 **Frame, analyze, and resolve problems using appropriate problem-solving techniques and decision-making skills.**

The situational leadership model teaches leaders to diagnose the needs of an individual or a team and then use the appropriate leadership style to respond to the needs of the person or group. Hersey and Blanchard (1988) characterized leadership style in terms of the amount of task behavior and relationship behavior that the leader provides to his or her followers. They categorized all leadership styles into four behavior types, which they named S1 to S4:

- S1: Telling—This type is characterized by one-way communication in which the leader defines the roles of the individual or group and provides the what, how, why, when, and where to do the task.
- S2: Selling—While the leader is still providing the direction, he or she is using two-way communication and providing the socio-emotional support that will allow the individual or group being influenced to buy into the process.
- S3: Participating—In this type, there is shared decision-making about aspects of how the task is accomplished and the leader is providing less task behavior while maintaining high relationship behavior.
- S4: Delegating—The leader is still involved in decisions; however, the process and responsibility has been passed to the individual or group. The leader stays involved to monitor progress.

Inevitably, problems occur in schools. How those problems are addressed and the quality of the problem-solving episode determines the longevity of the proposed solution and the probable reoccurrence of the same or similar difficulty.

Hersey and Blanchard (1988) identified four group problem-solving modes: (a) crisis mode, (b) organizational problem-solving mode, (c) interpersonal problem-solving mode, and (d) routine procedural mode. Using the situational leadership model, which emphasizes task behavior and relationship behavior, they described how each mode is used to resolve organizational problems.

When the crisis mode is used for problem solving, it requires high task behavior and low relationship behavior. When the organizational mode is applied, high task and high relationship behavior take place. The interpersonal mode suggests a high relationship and low task behavior. The routine mode uses low task and low relationship behavior.

Parnes, Noller, and Biondi (1977) developed a five-step model for problem solving. Their model provides for (a) fact finding, (b) problem finding, (c) idea finding, (d) solution finding, and (e) acceptance finding. Fact finding centers on gathering information related to a situation. The problem-finding step identifies the problems and subproblems. Idea finding employs techniques to create ideas about the problem. The solution-finding step uses criteria to evaluate the ideas.

Acceptance finding is the stage at which a plan of action is developed to address the problem.

Negotiation has become a central component of managing group conflict and improving group dynamics. For example, good leaders use "win-win" tactics that leave both sides in a conflict with an understanding that a decision was made in the best interest of both parties. Many other negotiation tactics have been found to be highly successful, and descriptions are available on the Internet.

Skill 7.4   Use strategies for promoting collaborative decision making and problem solving, facilitating team building, and developing consensus.

Collaborative leadership "requires a new notion of power . . . the more power we share, the more power we have to use" (http://www.collaborativeleadership.org/). It is the skillful and mission-driven management of important relationships. Collaborative leadership is the point at which organization and management come together. Collaborative leadership uses supportive and inclusive methods to ensure that all stakeholders affected by a decision are part of the change process.

Collaborative leaders must strive to build relationships with numerous stakeholders and create structures to support and sustain those relationships over time. There are several things that an effective principal can do to promote collaborative decision making and problem solving. First, it is important to identify the key stakeholders who will help reach the other stakeholders and decision makers. An effective team will be based on trusting, embracing conflict, remaining accountable, making a commitment to reach goals, and staying focused.

Second, the group must develop a shared vision. This shared vision should be based on a set of core beliefs to which all stakeholders can commit. This vision also incorporates the school district's vision and goals and the state standards. Paying attention and referring often to this shared vision throughout the change process is one of the most important ways for leaders to communicate effectively.

Developing Consensus

- Consensus is not the team leader imposing decisions and team members complying, as in a command situation.
- Consensus is not a perfect team agreement representing the first priorities of all team members. Everyone will not be totally happy with the consensus.
- Consensus is not a unanimous decision. This essentially gives each team member veto power.

- Consensus is not majority vote. This is faulty consensus, since it only reflects what the majority is happy with. The minority is forced to comply with a decision it doesn't want, which is not what consensus is about.
- Consensus is not "groupthink," the desire of cohesive teams to conform and make closed-minded decisions, disregarding critical examination, divergent opinions, or debate.
- Consensus is not a bland, watered-down proposal having no substance and entailing no risks.
- Effective consensus falls somewhere on a continuum between perfect agreement and total discord.

Some teams get bogged down trying to achieve perfect consensus, essentially giving each member veto power over any team decision, wasting time and provoking harmful interpersonal conflict. In other cases, teams find themselves at the other extreme—their search for consensus produces bland, watered-down initiatives that have little impact on strategic problems.

A consensus decision is one that all team members can support. It may be, but is not necessarily, the alternative most preferred by all members. When true consensus is reached through a process in which everyone participates, the output is usually a superior quality decision. Moreover, it is a decision having widespread acceptance and support for implementation. Most important, team members are motivated to see the decision through to completion (Brilhart and Galanes, 1989).

See also Skill 2.2.

Skill 7.5 Encourage and facilitate positive change, enlist support for change, and overcome obstacles to change.

Change is always easier to talk about than it is to accomplish. Yet change must be a consistent element of organizational vitality. Determining when to change and what to change in the organizational milieu presents difficulties for a leader. People resist change for a variety of reasons.

Perhaps the most prominent barrier to change is the threat it poses to individual roles and the perceived security individuals have in an organization. People resist change almost instinctively. Regardless of the way a certain task is being performed, individuals engaged in performing it are familiar with the details and comfortable using the existing format. Change is viewed as disruptive because members of an organization have devoted energy and resources to accomplishing certain tasks in prescribed ways. To alter the methodology used to accomplish the tasks engenders threat to competency—given a new way of doing it, individuals are not sure they can accomplish the task. Change entails the prospect of discarding the old way of doing something for a new way of doing it. So much has been invested in the old way that it can be difficult to acknowledge another method. In addition, there is a legitimacy of the old versus the unknown qualities of the new.

Proposed changes for the organization should be considered carefully. Several points serve as advice for a change agent. First, the change that is to be introduced should not be done abruptly, but rather mentioned and discussed over a period of time preceding its intended implementation. Considerable support for the change should be marshaled so that it has sufficient sustaining forces in the organization. Details regarding the specific goals that the change will address are important.

Furthermore, when change is top-down, or driven entirely be a school principal, for example, change is viewed as a threat. Successful change comes from allowing teachers in a school to be central in the decision-making and implementation process. While studies of decentralized decision making (or site-based management) are mixed on the impact of involving teachers in management decisions, in general principle, top-down imposed change causes more anxiety and is less effective at effecting real and significant change.

Doll (1996) discusses the process of change from three different perspectives. First, change is technical; that is, an innovation can be designed carefully and implemented into an organization with needed technical assistance. Second, change is political, meaning that there are special interests of individuals at work in the planning of change. Third, change is cultural. Each planned change has potential for disturbing or altering the cultural context.

The Northwest Regional Educational Laboratory used a modified version of the five classic steps in the change process in a plan called the *research utilizing problem-solving process.* Those steps are: (a) identifying a need for change, (b) diagnosing the situation in which change is to take place, (c) considering alternative courses of action, (d) testing the feasibility of a plan for change, and (e) adoption, diffusion, and adaptation of successful change effort. This plan presents one approach to the change process that concentrates on the initiation phase of a change process.

The change process is further complicated when there is no (or very little) existing support structure for the change or innovation to be introduced in the organization. Generally, a different kind of support system is necessary to maintain the change once it is introduced. It is important for a principal to be aware and to begin to develop a support system for change in the school environment. Teachers are the ones expected to implement innovations and sustain change in the school. For change to be successful, attention must be given to them and their emotional and professional needs regarding change. Neglecting teachers' emotional and professional needs creates difficulty with change or innovation. Change occurs best in a nonpunitive, low-pressure, supportive environment. School leaders who foster change on this basis increase the likelihood of change becoming legitimized in the school.

Skill 7.6 Apply skills for monitoring and evaluating change and making needed adjustments to achieve goals.

Typically, what gets monitored gets done. If no effort is made to collect and analyze information regarding the implemented change, the change most likely will lose its potential to succeed.

Effective school improvement processes are cyclical and continuous, with no clear beginning or end. Dr. Walter Shewhart (1939) developed the plan-do-study-act cycle for school improvement:

- Plan: Develop a plan for improvement.
- Do: Implement the plan.
- Study: Evaluate the impact according to specific criteria.
- Act: Adjust strategies to better meet criteria.

In spite of your good intentions, not every change will be successful as planned. At times, your efforts may not lead to the results you anticipated. But with rigorous measurement of your work, informed decision making, and a willingness to change, the improvement process can continue. When you gather data, you can adjust your practices, renew your plans, and try again. You can work to continuously improve.

Data are the key to continuous improvement. Focusing on data—rather than on intuition, tradition, or convenience—throughout the school improvement cycle has changed the way administrators and teachers make decisions.

When you plan, you must use data to provide insight and focus for your goals. Data patterns reveal strengths and weaknesses in the system and provide excellent direction. When you put the change into action, you *do*, and this generates additional data to study. Through collaborative reflection, you *study* the feedback offered by your data and begin to understand when to stay the course and when to make changes. Then, you *act* to refine your strategies. Then the cycle begins again.

The staff and other stakeholders must meet regularly to reflect on and reinforce the importance of the change. Meeting activities could include analyzing and sharing data, discussing problem-solving barriers and solutions, recognizing and celebrating staff and other stakeholders, sharing successful practices, and surveying staff and stakeholders for their awareness and understanding of the change effort. As schools monitor the effectiveness of a change effort, the next step is to determine whether adjustments are needed. The group can begin to refine some of the change strategies. At this point, that the school improvement cycle would begin again.

Classroom Walkthroughs

The practice of classroom observation and feedback has been one of the most commonly used tools in evaluating teacher performance, but classroom walkthroughs, for the purpose of professional development and monitoring and adapting to changes, has gained increasing popularity.

Instructional leadership is critical to the improvement of teaching and learning and plays a significant role in student achievement. For schools to respond and adapt, systems must exist that create the capacity to collectively process and apply knowledge about teaching and learning. Learning within a school is fostered when a group can identify a problem and create a plan to collectively solve it. The walkthrough model, derived from Hewlett-Packard's supervisory practice of Management by Wandering Around, has proven to be an effective and efficient way to collect data regarding instructional practices and provide feedback.

The classroom walkthrough model consists of a series of frequent classroom visits in which the observer(s) are present to look for predetermined evidence of specific practices. The observations last anywhere from 2 to 45 minutes and are intended to support the faculty in the delivery of instruction and curriculum.

According to the National Staff Development Council, walkthroughs provide the following opportunities:

- Reinforcing attention to instructional practices
- Gathering data about instructional practice and student learning
- Stimulating collegial conversation about teaching and learning
- Learning from other participants
- Deepening understandings and improving practices through continuous feedback
- Determining if change is being implemented as planned

Their greatest value is that administrators can use them to gather data, which can be used to prompt dialogue about instruction between teachers and administrators.

DOMAIN III.   ADMINISTRATIVE LEADERSHIP

COMPETENCY 8.0   **THE PRINCIPAL KNOWS HOW TO APPLY PRINCIPLES OF EFFECTIVE LEADERSHIP AND MANAGEMENT IN RELATION TO CAMPUS BUDGETING, PERSONNEL, RESOURCE UTILIZATION, FINANCIAL MANAGEMENT, AND TECHNOLOGY USE.**

Skill 8.1   **Apply procedures for effective budget planning and management.**

Principals must know basic accounting principles to provide appropriate fiscal management for the efficient economic operation of the school. Accounting is the process administrators use to record, present, summarize, and interpret accurate records of the financial data collected by the school through its daily operation. These basic accounting principles enable principals to evaluate the revenues and expenditures for the pre-established accounts of the school.

General principles of school cost accounting require using an accrual basis for accounting rather than a cash basis. This means that the financial transactions of the school must be recorded as revenues or expenditures at the time the transaction occurs and there should never be cash exchanged for goods or services. With accrual basis accounting, revenues earned at the time of the transaction become assets, and expenditures become liabilities, regardless of when the cash receipt or reimbursement occurs. Assets are inventory, investments, accounts receivable, building and fixed equipment, furniture, and motor vehicles; liabilities are salaries, benefits, accounts payable, and construction contracts. Unlike private, for-profit enterprises in which there is owners' equity, schools are owned by the taxpayers, and balances are known as fund equity, which includes reserves, retained earnings, and contributed capital.

Schools must adhere to specific rules governing their internal funds as prescribed by State Board Rules. All school organizations must be accountable for receipts and expenditures of funds obtained from the public. Additionally, sound business practices are expected for all financial transactions of the school. For example, in an effort to raise money to benefit school programs, fund-raising activities should not conflict with the programs administered by the school board.

All purchases from internal funds must be authorized by the principal or designee, and the district's preapproved, serially numbered receipt forms must be used to record any cash received and to record the accounting transaction. Each school must have a checking account, and each monthly statement must be reconciled as soon as it is received. Each account should have two authorized check signers, one being the principal. The principal should never pre-sign checks or purchase orders, under any circumstances. Monthly written financial reports must be made for the purpose of school decision making, and annual reports must be made for the district's annual financial statement.

The sponsors of classes, clubs, or department student activities (such as athletic events, musical performances, and the like) are responsible for providing the financial documents and records to the principal or designee. They must deposit money received in the school internal fund in the appropriate classified account (such as athletics, music, art, or Latin club). All disbursements by the club or organization must be made by check from internal funds. A financial report must be filed with the principal's office at the close of each fund-raising activity.

Records and documents of school financial transactions used for its internal fund and accounts must be examined periodically through the auditing process. This auditing process, whether internal or external, provides an adequate safeguard to preserve the property of the public school system. This process secures evidence of propriety of completed transactions; it determines whether all transactions have been recorded, whether these transactions have been accurately recorded in the appropriate accounts, and whether the statements have been drawn from the accounts.

Good auditing reviews are the result of excellent accounting practices. Drake and Roe (1994) define the accounting cycle as continuous and inclusive of the processes of documenting, analyzing, recording, and summarizing financial information. Documenting includes recording all financial transactions, including the authority or initiator of the transaction, ensuring that the debt incurred is within the limit of allotment, that every financial transaction is identified with a unit or fund, and that each fund is restrictive and limited in use. The process of analyzing requires that each transaction is analyzed and classified into debits and credits, and that each debit and credit is referenced to a specific account under the affected fund.

The school operation must always be conscious of its fiscal control to avoid overexpenditure and maintain a positive balance in each of its accounts. Therefore, an encumbrance system must be used to charge each purchase order, contract, or salary to an appropriation. Once paid, these transactions are canceled and cease to be an encumbrance as soon as the liability is recorded.

Future resources for education are planned through student enrollment forecasts. From the appropriated funds, the district builds its budget. At this point, the budget becomes an important device for translating the educational plan into a financial plan. The budget is, in effect, the translation of prioritized educational needs into a financial plan, which is interpreted for the public in such a way that when it is formally adopted, it expresses the kind of educational program the community is willing to support financially and morally for a one-year period (Drake and Roe, 1994).

The budget must be managed through a financial system of accounting. Revenues are categorized by sources. Sources of revenues can be federal, state, or local. Expenditures are categorized by dimensions, which include funds or account groups, objects, functions, facility, project, and reporting.

The funds or account groups are accounting entities with a self-balancing set of accounts that supports specific school activities to attain specific objectives. Therefore, funds or accounts can be used only for specified purposes.

At the school level, the district allots a certain number of dollars based on a predetermined local formula to allow expenditures from the general fund related to the day-to-day operation of the school. Additionally, the school may have an activity account and a school internal account. The activity account is derived from class fees, athletic contests and events, plays, yearly photos, and other special programs. While the proceeds belong to the school, they must be used for students' learning benefits such as award ribbons, trophies, and the like. These proceeds must be identified and accounted for in the same manner as any other school funds.

The school internal account usually originates from vending machine sales in the teachers' lounge and from related faculty activities and must be used to benefit faculty and staff. Again, these proceeds must be identified and accounted for in the same manner as any other school funds or accounts.

Skill 8.2 Work collaboratively with stakeholders to develop campus budgets.

The process for working collaboratively with stakeholders to create a campus budget is similar to the school improvement process. The principal should first gather information from as many stakeholders as possible, including certified and noncertified staff, parents, students, and other community members. Once that data has been collected, a school budget committee could be formed with representation from each of these groups.

The first goal of this committee should be to create a common vision. This vision should show a relationship between the school's budget and the school's improvement goals. Since all members of the committee may not be familiar with creating a school budget, it will be important to provide instruction for the members. Committee members should be provided with an explanation of the statutes that affect the school's budget. It also may be necessary to discuss the role of the stakeholders in the budget process. The principal may wish to share proposed budget allocations, curriculum needs and plans, and new programs and district initiatives. At that point, the principal should ask for input from the stakeholders and also present the data that was collected at the beginning of the process.

After the budget has been created, the committee may discuss ways to report expenditures throughout the school year. This may be done through monthly meetings or other communications, such as memos or emails.

The final step in the process is for the committee to present the proposed budget to the district for approval. If there are areas that are not approved, the committee should reconvene to make any necessary changes.

Skill 8.3 Acquire, allocate, and manage human, material, and financial resources according to district policies and campus priorities.

The management of resources at a school is a very difficult task. Principals are required not only to maintain budgets, but also to find funds from external sources; manage staffs of, on average, 20 to 100 teachers (in addition to support personnel); and keep track of material resources, such as office supplies, building materials, and instructional resources. How can a principal effectively do all this? Every district has specific policies and procedures. The first thing a new principal should do is learn those procedures. Where a principal has discretion, the principal should consider the school's mission and vision. When resources are not directed toward meeting the vision and mission of a school, those important elements are not cultivated or attended to. A principal can get the assistance of school personnel, parents, and other interested parties. When schools have site-based management committees, those groups often can represent various school needs that are affected by resource allocation.

After taking all those issues into account, as resources are allocated various procedures should be followed to keep track how things are done. For example, as staff is hired, principals can demonstrate alignment among the desired qualifications, the actual qualifications of the hired individual, the district policies, and the school's mission and vision. Doing this helps prevent concerns about decisions that are made.

The management of human, material, and financial resources requires careful documentation, clear policies, and effective communication. Resources of all types carry emotional and personal weight with school community members. Principals who forget about the political elements of running a school often find themselves having to repair relationships. Proactive principals consider all the political elements that might surface as decisions are made.

Skill 8.4 Apply laws and policies to ensure sound financial management in relation to accounts, bidding, purchasing, and grants.

The primary role of principals is improvement of student achievement, but they also are responsible for managing the campus finances. Principals must understand their campus budget in relation to the district's budget allocation and the rules and policies that regulate how schools may spend their funding. Because principals are not typically trained in accounting concepts, they often rely on bookkeepers or secretaries to maintain these records with little oversight. This lack of supervision can result in a loss of funds that can lead to loss of community trust and even the end of a principal's career.

What does a principal need to know about school finance? Every state has its own funding formula to allocate general distribution of funds to local districts to provide educational services to children. This formula usually is complex because of the efforts of state legislatures to provide uniformity of support. In most states, the funding for education comes from a blend of federal, state, and local revenues usually generated from taxes. Allegations that a system of funding based on taxes leads to disparity in property tax wealth among school systems have led to litigation. Federal and state mandates and policies have direct implications for school-level implementation of programs to meet the needs of children, especially when the level of funding is incongruent with the requirements of the law. Unfunded mandates put an unnecessary burden on local districts and schools and have led to an increase in local fund-raising for items necessary to carry on the business of the school. Helping legislators understand the financial implications of their programs or mandates at the district and campus level should be a priority for principals.

General accounting procedures are designed to meet three important school financial objectives: (1) to protect school staff from suspicion of theft, (2) to protect school assets, and (3) to fulfill the public's expectation that public funds will be spent responsibly. The use of school activity funds is restricted, which means that the funds are not yours to lend, borrow, or spend in any way you like. You must follow the following principles:

- You may use the funds only for the purpose for which those funds have been raised.
- If funds have been raised by the entire student body, then they must be spent to benefit the entire student body.
- If students are old enough, students should have representation, with faculty supervision, in the management and spending of the funds raised by the student group.
- Activity funds should be spent on the students who were in school at the time the funds were raised.
- Fund-raising projects should not conflict with or detract from the instructional program or put students in an unsafe situation. Many schools restrict students from door-to-door sales due to concerns for student safety.
- Activity funds should be managed with sound accounting procedures, including the use of receipts for all funds received.

There are several types of internal controls that assist a principal in overseeing the appropriate spending of campus funds. The policy of having principals approve all purchase orders will prevent misuse of funds. Having the principal review the monthly bank statements helps detect errors and incongruities in spending practices. If an error is found, the principal can follow up with the bank. Bookkeepers should be restricted to working only when an administrator is in the building. Relying on one person with little or no supervision is a recipe for trouble. If a principal fails to place and maintain reasonable financial controls, then he or she may unknowingly become an ally to dishonest employees.

See also Skill 8.1.

Skill 8.5 Use effective planning, time management, and organization of personnel to maximize attainment of district and campus goals.

Principals are required to make quick decisions and react to numerous problems and situations throughout every school day. Some days it seems as though all principals can do is wait for what and who is going to come at them next. In the process, they feel like someone who has the responsibility to lead, but hasn't been given the authority to think, decide, and take action.

Proactivity is one of the most popular management buzzwords to come from the 1990s. Stephen Covey, who has "be proactive" as the first of his famous *7 Habits of Highly Effective People,* defines proactivity as more than merely taking the initiative, but focuses on "response-ability"—the ability and freedom to choose a response to a stimulus. Look at the model below, which show the difference between reactive thinking, in which a stimulus gives rise to an immediate response, and proactivity, in which there is sufficient space between the stimulus and the response for an individual to choose a response.

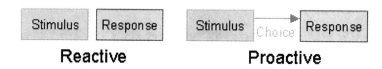

Reactive   Proactive

The key to this model is recognizing and using the space between stimulus and response to make responsible choices by calling upon self-awareness, imagination, conscience, and independent will. Proactive leadership springs from awareness that we are not a product of our systems or our environments. Those things powerfully influence us, but we can choose our responses to them. The two marks of proactive leadership are the ability to anticipate and meet the future and the ability to respond intentionally and freely.

Good leaders get all the facts possible on all sides of an issue prior to making a decision, unless the situation requires immediate action. At times, a leader must react to be successful. However, if the predominant leadership stance is reacting, leading will not be productive or satisfying. Today's effective principals look at their responsibilities holistically, not as a series of tasks and responses to emergencies.

See also Skill 7.1.

Skill 8.6 Develop and implement plans for using technology and information systems to enhance school management.

Information is a critical resource in the operation and management of organizations. Timely availability of relevant information is vital for effective performance of managerial functions such as planning, organizing, leading, and control. An information system in an organization is like the nervous system in the human body: it is the link that connects all the organization's components and provides for better operation and survival in a competitive environment. Indeed, today's organizations run on information.

The term *information system* usually refers to a computer-based system that is designed to support the operations, management, and decision functions of an organization. Information systems in organizations thus provide information support for decision makers. Information systems encompass transaction processing systems, management information systems, decision support systems, and strategic information systems.

Information consists of data that have been processed and are meaningful to a user. A system is a set of components that operate together to achieve a common purpose. Thus a management information system collects, transmits, processes, and stores data about an organization's resources, programs, and accomplishments. The system makes possible the conversion of these data into management information for use by decision makers within the organization.

The last few decades have witnessed the debut of a number of electronic devices under the heading of school technology. Each of these devices has particular capabilities and advantages, that when applied in the interactive experience of teaching and learning, make the process stimulating, relevant, and constructive. When these electronic tools are applied to administrative tasks, they facilitate efficiency and increase productivity.

Since technology is expensive to acquire and maintain, it is important that the introduction of given technological devices addresses specific school goals and objectives. Technology can make a number of administrative tasks quicker and more efficient. Tasks such as scheduling, accounting, purchasing, inventory, attendance, grading, testing, and library functions can benefit. The appropriate use of technology in these areas can make a difference in personal productivity, efficiency, and time expenditure. A principal's ability to identify the capabilities of technological devices and to match that technology with the needs, goals, and objectives of the school's curriculum and administrative functions is a primary skill.

A database is a collection of programs that store and retrieve large amounts of information. Every school district and school building needs a way to track data that is collected for its district, state, and federal governance. Schools can effectively maintain records of students' data, including grades, schedules, absences, demographics, test scores, behavior, and medical records.

Schools need a way to collect data and print out reports using this data for evaluation purposes. The software needed for the school/student management purpose needs to be efficient and at the fingertips of administration. At any time, the parent, school board, or government can request information that is provided by the school's management system. A management system can hold test scores, which allow schools and teachers to see trends. If new techniques are used to improve learning, a management system can show the rise in test scores that validates the effectiveness of the technique.

Another aspect in which IS plays a large roll as a management tool is scheduling. Scheduling classes for a school of 400 high school students could be a nightmare if it had to be done by hand. Computer software can store students' preferences or abilities in a database. When the schedule is created for the next school year, the database can be used to place students in the appropriate classes.

The software application Administrator's Plus, developed by Rediker Software, collects the budget data that a school sets up and tracks the spending of the money. At any time, a year-to-date expenditures versus budget report can be produced. This prevents overspending and improves accurate allocations of monies to various departments.

The acquisition of software is expensive. Mistakes in the selection of software programs prevent the school from accomplishing intended objectives. Software evaluation is a critical skill for administrators. Administrators should follow these steps when selecting software:

- Identify the objectives that are to be accomplished by introducing the software in the school environment.
- Determine if the features and capabilities of the software match administrative goals and objectives.
- Determine if the software actually does what it describes and if what it does is what is needed.
- Be sure to ascertain that the software is compatible with the computer system in operation at the school.

New technology brings with it considerations of privacy and confidentiality of group and individual information. It is important to determine who should and should not have access to certain records. Security is always an issue when significant amounts of information are stored in one location. Enormous amounts of information are stored on computers, and that information is often sensitive and not for general dissemination. Public use of student data breaches professional ethics. The confidentiality of school records is paramount. In this time of security breaches, the security of school records becomes a high priority. Computers with school records also are susceptible to computer viruses. Principals must be vigilant and ensure that security software is installed and kept up to date on school computers.

COMPETENCY 9.0   THE PRINCIPAL KNOWS HOW TO APPLY PRINCIPLES OF LEADERSHIP AND MANAGEMENT TO THE CAMPUS PHYSICAL PLANT AND SUPPORT SYSTEMS TO ENSURE A SAFE AND EFFECTIVE LEARNING ENVIRONMENT.

Skill 9.1   Implement strategies that enable the school physical plant, equipment, and support systems to operate safely, efficiently, and effectively.

School leaders are charged with providing students a safe, efficient, comfortable school building, conducive to rigorous academic learning. While school districts and funding levels play significant parts in the aesthetics of a school building, basic safety and comfort issues are the responsibility of a school's administrative team. Various strategies can be put into place to promote satisfactory levels of building safety and efficiency.

A principal—or a designee, such as an assistant principal—should be responsible on a daily basis to make rounds on a campus to verify a checklist of items. Such items might include visiting restrooms to ensure that everything is working properly and that students have clean, well-operating facilities to use. A checklist might also include examining blacktop in the athletic areas to ensure that students would be safe running or playing on outside surfaces.

The principal must also advocate for building comforts at the district and community level. For example, while not all districts can afford air conditioning, principals can make needs clear to local taxpayers (with superintendent approval).

Many school districts pay for utilities, and school building leaders can examine utility usage for efficiency. They may note problems in terms of air drafts, heating duct problems, and plumbing.

Finally, school leaders should report problems that pose safety or privacy concerns to the district buildings manager. For example, if a bathroom stall door does not work properly, either a building-level custodian must fix it or, if the building-level resources are not available, a district support staff member should fix it. The same is true for issues of safety, such as a ceiling panel that is about to fall off in a classroom.

Skill 9.2 **Apply strategies for ensuring the safety of students and personnel and for addressing emergencies and security concerns.**

Schools must be safe places for students to learn and for teachers to work. When emergencies occur, clear procedures must be in place to ensure that the school community responds in an orderly fashion. Details for creating and implementing safety plans are explained in Skill 9.3.

First, the building must be in an operable condition. Any broken item that could pose a safety risk should be dealt with. Furniture that gets in the way of door areas must be moved. All doors should be completely operable and able to be opened quickly in an emergency. Windows should be able to be opened. Air conditioners, heaters, gas systems, plumbing, and electricity should all be able to be turned off easily and quickly if the need arises. This last point is a particular concern for many schools. If a specific custodian knows how to complete all those procedures, other individuals also need to learn how to operate such equipment in the case of that custodian's absence.

In planning for evacuation, routes should be drawn so that each hallway has the smallest possible number of students walking through it, with no student having to walk too far. The quickest route out of a building may clog a hallway, thereby making the route much slower. Often, fire departments or safety consultants can assist in designing solid, quality evacuation plans.

A lockdown plan is the opposite of an evacuation plan and consists of various rules and procedures for getting or keeping all students in a secure location, such as a classroom. Often communication suffers during a lockdown, so many schools now insist that school personnel look at their email accounts as soon as a lockdown occurs to give the administration an efficient way to communicate to many people quickly.

Overall, the best way to keep students and staff safe is careful planning. It is crucial that all school community members know those plans well and practice them often.

Skill 9.3 **Develop and implement procedures for crisis planning and for responding to crises.**

To ensure student and personnel safety, principals must implement various levels of planning. There must be plans for ensuring safety in a variety of situations.

To enhance school safety, the Department of Homeland Security offers funding, training, and resources, such as providing money for emergency preparedness, training school bus drivers in security, and hardening school buildings' vulnerability. Federal Emergency Management Agency (FEMA) assistance includes funding, training and exercises, equipment testing, and Citizen Corps. FEMA's Emergency Management Institute offers free online courses to train school officials to prepare for and manage emergencies. Plans must account for local natural disasters and for ensuring safety when, for example, the police are searching for a criminal in the surrounding neighborhood.

Preparedness

Good planning will facilitate a rapid, coordinated, effective response when a crisis occurs. Determine what crisis plans exist in the district, school, and community.

- Identify all stakeholders involved in crisis planning.
- Develop procedures for communicating with staff, students, families, and the media.
- Establish procedures to account for students during a crisis.
- Gather information about the school facility, such as maps and the location of utility shutoffs.
- Identify the equipment that needs to be assembled to assist staff in a crisis.

Plans should include methods for getting students in a safe area and communication among staff members and between administrative personnel and parents or media.

The plans must be communicated to staff, parents, students, and the district. Fire drills, for example, do not command great attention from most staff and students, typically because most people have never experienced a fire in a large institution. However, good administrators find creative ways to ensure that all staff members and students know the procedures. Clear directions should be posted all over a campus for clarification when events occur. Directions and procedures should be mailed home to parents annually, as well.

Response

A crisis is the time to follow the crisis plan and make use of your preparations.

- Determine if a crisis is occurring.
- Identify the type of crisis that is occurring and determine the appropriate response.
- Activate the incident management system.
- Ascertain whether an evacuation, reverse evacuation, lockdown, or shelter-in-place needs to be implemented.
- Maintain communication among all relevant staff at officially designated locations.

- Establish what information needs to be communicated to staff, students, families, and the community.
- Monitor how emergency first aid is being administered to the injured.
- Decide if more equipment and supplies are needed.

When disasters or safety concerns occur, school leaders must behave like flight attendants: calm and collected, but decisive and clear. People in the school community will behave in a positive, productive manner during an emergency when the leadership gives clear instructions, is open and honest, and maintains a sense of peace while acting decisively.

Recovery
During recovery, return to learning and restore the infrastructure as quickly as possible.

- Strive to return to learning as quickly as possible.
- Restore the physical plant and the school community.
- Monitor how staff are assessing students for the emotional impact of the crisis.
- Identify what follow-up interventions are available to students, staff, and first responders.
- Conduct debriefings with staff and first responders.
- Assess curricular activities that address the crisis.
- Allocate appropriate time for recovery.
- Plan how anniversaries of events will be commemorated.
- Capture "lessons learned" and incorporate them into revisions and trainings.

Skill 9.4   Apply local, state, and federal laws and policies to support sound decision making related to school programs and operations (e.g., student services, food services, health services, transportation).

Title VI of the Civil Rights Act of 1964 extends protection against discrimination on the basis of race, color, or national origins in any program or activity receiving federal financial assistance (*Clark v. Huntsville, Tyler v. Hot Springs*).

Title VII of the Civil Rights Act of 1964 states that it is unlawful for an employer to discriminate against any individual with respect to compensation, terms, conditions, or privileges of employment because of an individual's race, color, religion, sex, or national origin. Some exceptions are noted in this statute. It does not apply to religious organizations that seek individuals of a particular religion to perform the work of that organization. Where suspect classifications (those classifications having no basis in rationality) represent bona fide occupational qualifications, they are permitted. Classifications based upon merit and seniority are also acceptable under this statute (*Ansonia BOE v. Philbrook*).

Title IX of the Education Amendments of 1972 states that no individual shall be excluded from participation in, be denied the benefits of, or be subjected to discrimination under any educational program or activity that receives or benefits from federal assistance on the basis of sex. This statute covers the areas of admission, education programs and activities, access to course offerings, counseling and the use of appraisal and counseling materials, marital or parental status, and athletics (*Marshall v. Kirkland*).

Section 504 of the Rehabilitation Act of 1973 indicates that "No otherwise handicapped individual . . . will be excluded from the participation in, be denied the benefits of, or be subjected to discrimination under any program or activity receiving federal financial assistance solely because of his/her handicap (*School Board of Nassau County v. Arline*).

The Age Discrimination Act of 1967 states that it shall be unlawful for an employer to fail or refuse to hire or discharge any individual or otherwise discriminate against any individual with respect to his or her employment because of an individual's age. This statute does allow an employer or employment to consider age as a bone fide occupational qualification (bfoq) (*Geller v. Markham*).

The Family Rights and Privacy Act of 1964 (FERPA) [Buckley Amendment] states that no funds will be made available under any applicable program to any state or local educational agency, any institution of higher education, any community college, any school, any agency offering a preschool program, or any other educational institution that has a policy of denying parents of students the right to inspect and review any and all official records, files, and data directly related to their children. This includes material incorporated into the student's cumulative folder such as identifying data, academic work completed, level of achievement, attendance date, testing results, health data, family background information, teacher or counselor ratings and observations, and verified reports of serious or recurring behavior problems. Each educational organization must establish appropriate procedures for granting access requests within a reasonable period of time (not to exceed 45 days).

- Parents have an opportunity for a hearing to challenge the record's contents, to ensure the record's accuracy, and to provide corrected or rebuttal information.
- Educational organizations must require written consent of the parent to release identifying information to external individuals and organizations. (The state specifies exceptions.)
- All persons, agencies, or organizations seeking access to a student's record must sign a written form that must be included in the student file.

- Students who are 18 years of age or attending a postsecondary educational institution acquire the right of consent formerly held by the parent. Directory information can be released without consent. Such information includes the following: student's name, address, telephone listing, date and place of birth, major field of study, participation in officially recognized activities and sports, weight and height of members of athletic teams, dates of attendance, degrees and awards of attendance, degrees and awards received, and the most recent educational agency or institution attended by the student.

Student records may be protected simultaneously by laws administered by the U.S. Department of Education and by other state and federal agencies. FERPA establishes a high level of privacy protection, but statutes administered by agencies within the U.S. Departments of Agriculture, Health and Human Services, and Justice also protect records privacy and may apply to the records of students in schools. Professional standards of ethical practice, under which school doctors and nurses, psychologists, and other professionals operate, may also establish privacy restrictions. Following are some examples:

- Information about students certified eligible for free and reduced-price school meals is covered by confidentiality restrictions administered by the U.S. Department of Agriculture.
- Records of drug and alcohol prevention and treatment services for students are covered by confidentiality restrictions administered by the U.S. Department of Health and Human Services.

The Individuals with Disabilities Education Act (IDEA) requires that states adopt policies that assure all children with disabilities receive a "free and appropriate public education." The statute requires that each student's unique needs are addressed through an individualized educational plan (IEP) and that extensive procedural requirements are put into place. Requirements allow for the withholding of federal financial resources to states that fail to comply with the statute (*Honig v. Doe, Hendrick Hudson Board of Education v. Rowley*).

The Equal Access Act of 1985 states that it will be unlawful for any public secondary school which receives federal financial assistance and which has a limited open forum to deny equal access or a fair opportunity to or discriminate against any students who wish to conduct a meeting within that limited open forum on the basis of the religious, political, philosophical, or other content of the speech at the meetings. A limited open forum exists whenever a school grants an opportunity for one or more non-curriculum-related student groups to meet on the school premises during noninstructional time. The criteria for a fair opportunity provide that:
- the meeting is voluntary and student initiated;
- there is no sponsorship by the school, the government, or its agents or employees;

- school agents or employees are present at the meetings only in a nonparticipatory capacity;
- the meeting does not substantially interfere with the orderly conduct of educational activities within the school; and
- nonschool persons may not direct, conduct, control, or regularly attend activities of student groups.

This statute authorizes the school, its agents, or employees to maintain order and discipline on the school premises, to protect the well-being of students and faculty, and to ensure that the attendance of the students at the meeting is voluntary (*Board of Education of Westside Community Schools v. Mergens*).

The federal constitutional amendments cited contain powerful clauses, and educators must ensure that a balance is struck between the individual's constitutional freedoms and the state's compelling interest (that is, to provide an appropriate educational environment).

Court cases that arise out of the federal constitution and/or federal statutes come under the jurisdiction of the federal court system. As noted earlier, when school administrators, teachers, and school employees act in their official capacities, they represent the state. This has significant implications for analyzing actions performed in the course of official duties that could breach the constitutional and statutory rights of students, parents, teachers, and staff members.

The Congress of the United States and state legislatures have the authority to attack discrimination by passing statutes that codify constitutional intent and even surpass that intent as long as the statutes do not violate the equal protection rights of others. Congressional statutes provide broader equal opportunity rights and remedies by linking the observation of those rights to federal dollars, by prohibiting acts that are not covered by the Constitution, and by creating remedies that are not available under the Constitution. The evidentiary requirements to establish statutory discrimination are lower than those required for constitutional discrimination (Valente, 1994, p. 336).

SAMPLE TEST: SUBTEST I – SCHOOL COMMUNITY LEADERSHIP

Directions: Read each item and select the best response.

1. The demographics have markedly changed over the past few years for the neighborhood from which the students at Jones High School come. The single-family homes are now occupied by multiple families. The first language of most adults has changed from English to Spanish. The businesses in the community are also changing and are requiring different types of skilled employees. You, as principal, have been asked to redesign your program to better meet the businesses' labor needs. Your first step to meet these needs is to:
(Skill 1.2) (Average)

   A. Talk to the new residents at a town meeting you establish at the school

   B. Conduct a survey of the business owners to determine their needs

   C. Plan to enlarge the school to meet increased student enrollment

   D. Discuss the matter with your area supervisor

2. What must become the norm for teachers to improve teaching and learning?
(Skill 1.3) (Rigorous)

   A. Higher pay

   B. Time to work alone with their students

   C. Better training on

   D. Time to plan with colleagues

3. Which area does a good education benefit most?
(Skill 1.4) (Average)

   A. Individuals enjoy a higher standard of living

   B. Society has a skilled workforce that stimulates economic growth

   C. Both A and B ✓

   D. Neither A nor B

4. What does a principal need before writing a strategic plan?
(Skill 1.5) (Rigorous)

   A. All necessary information

   B. Identification of a problem or need

   C. A commitment to action

   D. None of the above

5. Which of the following student achievement data should be used in formulating the school's strategic plan?
(Skill 1.5) (Average)

A. STAAR test results

B. District benchmarks

C. Classroom assessments

D. All of the above

6. Smith Elementary School is on the critically low list for the second year. About 90% of the students are on free and reduced lunches. Most live in the public housing project in single-parent homes. Strategies used last year did not significantly improve student achievement. To change this school, you would:
(Skill 1.6) (Rigorous)

A. Have an initial session with a consultant and the teachers to determine how to proceed before developing a plan

B. Seek to involve more parents in the education of their children

C. Meet with the teachers and develop new strategies

D. Form a small committee to establish what should be done

7. The state has put your school on the critically low school list. No measurable gains were recorded the second year, and you are on the list two consecutive years. How would you get your school off the list?
(Skill 1.6) (Average)

A. Involve the community

B. Have a meeting with teachers and establish a strategic plan that involves the parents and community

C. Secure advice from the state and district and work on the problem

D. Conduct a series of meetings with teachers, students, parents, and community members to obtain information in developing a plan of action with the faculty

8. **Recommended practice suggests that which of the following should be involved in the decision-making process concerning school improvement?**
(Skill 1.6) (Easy)

   I. Teachers
   II. Community partners
   III. Administration
   IV. Parents and students

A. I and III only

B. II and III only

C. I, III, and IV only

D. I, II, III, and IV

9. **Which of the following best describes the process of school planning?**
(Skill 1.7) (Average)

A. The visionary principal, who knows about the needs of the school, develops the school plan

B. Principal, teachers, parents, business partners, and other community members develop the school plan

C. Principals, teachers, and parents develop the school plan

D. A visionary team of teachers and administrators develops the school plan

10. **Which of the following should mark the initial stages of school-based planning?**
(Skill 1.7) (Easy)

A. Developing a plan of action

B. Evaluating the process

C. Clarifying and articulating the mission and goals

D. Analyzing the plan of action

11. A logical sequence in formulating goals is _____.
(Skill 1.7) (Easy)

A. Philosophy, aims, goals, objectives

B. Philosophy, goals, aims, objectives

C. Aims, philosophy, objectives, goals

D. Philosophy, aims, objectives, goals

12. Which of the following best illustrates an educational goal?
(Skill 1.7) (Average)

A. Provide good health and physical fitness

B. By the year 2018, the high school graduation rate will increase to at least 90%

C. Develop self-realization

D. The students will complete a reading comprehension examination within 30 minutes with 80% accuracy

13. Technological resources are limited in the school. The teacher in the Technology Lab does not want anyone else to use the equipment without her permission and supervision. Several teachers could operate the laboratory in an efficient manner. The best policy statement for the principal to make is to:
(Skill 1.8) (Rigorous)

A. Require the technology teacher to permit others to use the lab as long as they adhere to lab policies and meet the mission of the school

B. Enforce the procedures established by the technology teacher

C. Assign another teacher to the technology lab

D. Get the teachers to reach an agreement

14. A teacher has asked the principal for funds to attend a conference on autism, the librarian has asked for additional library books, and the coach wants new football uniforms. How does a principal decide which request is approved?
(Skill 1.8) (Rigorous)

A. Look at the school improvement plan

B. Seek guidance from the CPOC

C. Allow the teaching staff to vote on the spending proposals.

D. Both A and B

15. During the induction process, the principal should ensure that the new teacher receives information about:
(Skill 1.9) (Easy)

A. The school mission

B. Students who misbehave

C. Outdated policy handbooks

D. Parent attitudes

16. Student achievement scores have decreased. What is information that a principal must consider to improve student achievement?
(Skill 1.10) (Rigorous)

A. Each teacher's results

B. Each student's results

C. What did not work

D. Both A and B

17. The principal of Bestever High School wants to create a Wall of Fame of photos of outstanding volunteers. This is an example of which principal competency?
(Skill 1.11) (Average)

A. Acknowledge and celebrate the contributions of students, parents, and community members toward realization of the campus vision

B. Support innovative thinking and risk taking within the school community

C. Develop and implement strategies for effective internal and external communication

D. Develop and implement a comprehensive program of community relations that effectively involves and informs multiple constituencies, including the media.

18. Which of the following statements best describes the position method for studying community power structure?
(Skill 2.1) (Average)

A. Persons who hold the highest position in formal organizations are the community leaders

B. Individuals who patronize the local population by distributing rewards and jobs are the community leaders

C. Community leadership is based entirely on who has the most money

D. Community leadership is based entirely on interlocking organizations and the relative power individuals can acquire as members of numerous organizations

19. One method used in studying a community's power structure is comprised of the following steps. One, select several decision areas. Two, conduct in-depth interviews. Three, analyze documentary evidence. Identify this technique.
(Skill 2.1) (Easy)

A. Critical inquiry method

B. Decision analysis technique

C. Reputational technique

D. Comparative analysis technique

20. Mrs. Jones has just been appointed the new principal at the local high school. New to the area, she decides to conduct a community power structure study. First, she asks people who know the community for a list of individuals prominent in business, government, and civic affairs. Next, she asks a panel of people who know community affairs to select the most prominent of the leaders. Third, she interviews each person identified by the panel. Then, she analyzes the data to provide a view of the community power structure. Identify the technique used in her study of the community power structure.
(Skill 2.1) (Rigorous)

A. Comparative analysis technique

B. Critical inquiry method

C. Structured analysis model

D. Reputational technique

21. **A type of community power structure is termed *amorphous*. Which of the following statements is an accurate description of this type of structure?**
    (Skill 2.1) (Rigorous)

    A. This power structure is characterized by a single group of individuals who make major decisions

    B. This power structure is characterized by multiple groups positioning for decision-making power

    C. This power structure is characterized by various groups from at least two communities having a common goal

    D. This power structure is characterized by an absence of a pattern of individuals or groups making decisions

22. **Carver and Crowe summarized four basic community power structures as pyramidal or monolithic, caucus or factional, coalitional or polylithic, and amorphous. Which of the following statements best describes a factional or caucus power structure?**
    (Skill 2.1) (Rigorous)

    A. There is a relatively stable and predictable power structure

    B. Multiple groups and organizations elicit and impart power to the community based upon their interests

    C. Two or more groups vie for decision-making power

    D. Citizen input dominates decision making

23. Because schools are open systems and operate within a community environment, a school with an effective community relations program and a positive image may be more effective in:
(Skill 2.1) (Easy)

A. Obtaining federal grants to support school programs

B. Securing support from the community to carry out projects

C. Being selected to appear on television programs

D. Sending more of its graduates to college

24. Which of the following statements best describes the competitive elite power structure?
(Skill 2.1) (Rigorous)

A. A group or groups of leaders who dominate community policies

B. A group that is non-innovative and opposed to change

C. A group concerned with ideological differences

D. A group that embraces an open process of decision making

25. Which of the following statements best describes the monopolistic community power structure?
(Skill 2.1) (Average)

A. A group or groups of leaders who dominate community policies

B. A group that is non-innovative or opposed to change

C. A group concerned with ideological differences

D. A group that embraces an open process of decision making

26. **Research on teacher participation in decision making reveals that teachers' involvement in formulating policies is an important factor in morale. The question that arises is: Under what conditions should subordinates be involved in decision-making? Which of the following statements best demonstrates an acceptable approach?**
   (Skill 2.2) (Average)

   A. Apply the test of relevance, which asks if subordinates have a personal stake in decision outcomes, and the test of expertise, which asks if subordinates have the expertise to contribute to a decision

   B. When it appears that the decision-making process will be victimized by the group-think syndrome, invite subordinates to participate in the decision-making process

   C. After preliminary consensus is reached, then invite subordinates to participate in the decision-making process

   D. Once the decision-making cycle has been completed and the possible outcomes predicted, then involve subordinates in the decision-making process

27. **The first step in using good group persuasive techniques is to:**
   (Skill 2.2) (Easy)

   A. Plan an in-depth report of facts and statistics to support your argument

   B. Analyze the biases, emotions, and interests of the group to be addressed

   C. Make an impassioned, emotional appeal

   D. Solicit listener opinion before stating your objective

28. **The appropriate administrator completes the master plan of teaching assignments for the coming school year in time to notify teachers of their assignments before the current school year ends. This step will increase teacher morale if:**
   (Skill 2.2) (Rigorous)

   A. The plan is published so they can make lesson-planning adjustments during the summer

   B. Its purpose is to solicit feedback to make changes satisfactory to most teachers

   C. Last-minute changes have to be made before school opens

   D. Teachers know that the administration is acting in good faith

29. You are a new principal in a school in which 95% of the faculty has been on staff during your previous five-year tenure as assistant principal at the same site. Grapevine says that during faculty meetings you speak in half sentences and frequently make reference to events and situations with which only long-time teachers are familiar. You should:
(Skill 2.3) (Rigorous)

A. Bring a larger group into your inner circle

B. Allow teachers to ask clarification questions

C. Continue to seek grapevine feedback

D. Speak to teachers about their problems decoding your presentations

30. Which of the following represents the proper sequence of the communication process?
(Skill 2.3) (Easy)

A. Ideating, decoding, transmitting, receiving, encoding, acting

B. Ideating, encoding, transmitting, receiving, decoding, acting

C. Ideating, transmitting, encoding, receiving, decoding, acting

D. Ideating, encoding, transmitting, receiving, acting, decoding

31. Communication in which a school principal receives feedback from the faculty/staff is:
(Skill 2.4) (Average)

A. Downward

B. Lateral

C. Upward

D. Diagonal

32. Which of the following is _not_ true of the educational grapevine? *(Skill 2.4) (Rigorous)*

A. It is the least reliable source of transmitting information

B. It is the means by which most information is passed laterally among employees

C. Its most negative feature is the transmission of unsubstantiated rumor

D. It can be used effectively by administrators to test employee reactions that facilitate the decision-making process

33. Who needs to communicate well in a school? *(Skill 2.5) (Easy)*

A. The principal

B. The teachers

C. The parents

D. All of the above

34. If a principal wants students to achieve higher grades and test scores, he or she must provide: *(Skill 2.6) (Rigorous)*

A. After-school tutorials

B. Summer school

C. Opportunities for parents to be involved

D. Data analysis training

35. Which of the following statements describes responsibilities of today's principal? *(Skill 3.1) (Average)*

A. A principal's behavior, stated communication, and implied communication have a tremendous impact on those around him or her

B. A principal must resolve conflict in a systematic, fair manner and promote this behavior in others

C. A principal is responsible for maintaining a positive perception of the school and must control negative information about all aspects of the school

D. All of the above

36. Which of the following set of topics best describes the Revised Code of Ethics and Standard Practices for Texas Educators?
(Skill 3.2) (Average)

A. Ethical guidelines for accepting gifts, record keeping, and professional relationships

B. Confidentiality, misappropriation of funds, and litigation

C. Personal conduct, conduct toward colleagues, and conduct toward students

D. Political, fiscal, and ethical responsibilities

37. The Individuals with Disabilities Education Act (IDEA) was enacted to:
(Skill 3.4) (Average)

A. Ensure students overcome language barriers that impede equal participation in instructional programs

B. Provide equal educational opportunities for students regardless of race, color, or national origin

C. Improve accountability, expand services, simplify parental involvement, and provide earlier access to services and supports for students with special needs

D. Ensure confidentiality of records and other information about students, parents, or staff members with disabilities

38. Since participating in our democratic society is critical for the future of our country, what can Principal Martinez do to prepare students to be responsible, active citizens? *(Skill 3.6) (Rigorous)*

A. Choose a curriculum that emphasizes ethical principles, moral values, and civic participation

B. Expose students to role models who have achieved success and personally demonstrate responsible behavior

C. Promote the continuous and appropriate development of all students

D. All of the above

39. Principals have a responsibility to act as _____ for the children they serve every day. *(Skill 3.7) (Easy)*

A. Advocates

B. Disciplinarians

C. Teachers

D. Coaches

40. What should a principal who is new to a school do to promote necessary change? *(Skill 3.8) (Average)*

A. Identify areas of need and thoroughly research new programs that could alleviate the problem

B. Spend a short time observing school procedures and make the most important changes immediately

C. Involve teachers and other stakeholders in the planning and development process

D. Impose ideas, because many teachers are afraid of change and will not cooperate unless an authority figure requires their participation

41. Which of the following strategies is _least_ likely to cause students to embrace diversity?
(Skill 3.9) (Rigorous)

A. Provide opportunities for students to share their life experiences and cultures

B. Strive to make all students and parents feel welcome and included in every aspect of the school community

C. Depend on teachers and textbooks to provide an accurate and comprehensive global vision

D. Build a school culture based on a foundation of respect and high expectations

42. Ms. Martinez teaches World Geography at a high school in which 60% of the students are Hispanic, 20% are African American, and 20% are European American. Which would be the best project for her to assign to start the school year if she wants to benefit from the diversity of her students?
(Skill 3.9) (Rigorous)

A. Give each student a map of the world on which to identify and color a list of countries; she will then display the maps

B. Have students work in homogeneous groups and compare the similarities and differences of their parents' families

C. Give an overview of the semester's objectives, assign the first chapter of the textbook, and have students work in groups to compare their answers to the questions at the end of the chapter

D. Have each student locate his or her family's country(ies) by placing a color-coded pin on a large world map; have students share a story about their family's coming to the United States with the entire class

ANSWER KEY: SUBTEST I – SCHOOL COMMUNITY LEADERSHIP

1. B	15. A	29. B
2. D	16. C	30. B
3. C	17. A	31. C
4. B	18. A	32. A
5. D	19. B	33. D
6. A	20. D	34. C
7. D	21. D	35. D
8. D	22. C	36. C
9. B	23. B	37. C
10. C	24. C	38. D
11. A	25. A	39. A
12. B	26. A	40. C
13. A	27. B	41. C
14. D	28. B	42. D

RIGOR TABLE: SUBTEST I—SCHOOL COMMUNITY LEADERSHIP

Easy	Average	Rigorous		
21%	38%	41%		
10, 15, 19, 23, 27, 30, 33, 35, 39	1, 3, 5, 7, 8, 9, 11, 12, 17, 24, 25, 26, 31, 32, 36, 37	2, 4, 6, 13, 14, 16, 18, 20, 21, 22, 28, 29, 34, 38, 40, 41, 42		

SAMPLE TEST: SUBTEST II – INSTRUCTIONAL LEADERSHIP
Directions: Read each item and select the best response

1. _____ is the process of gathering information to identify and define the problem before initiating a project or program. *(Skill 4.1) (Easy)*

   A. Surveying

   B. Needs assessment

   C. Evaluation

   D. Aims and goals identification

2. **Effective teacher involvement in a new program is highly dependent on _____.** *(Skill 4.1) (Rigorous)*

   A. Teacher satisfaction with the curriculum planners' background

   B. District office politics concerning program planning and development

   C. Teacher involvement in the planning process and in-service training

   D. Parent and community buy-in to the design of the program and evaluation process

3. **Which of the following is an approach that sees the curriculum as emergent and concerned with cultivating the processes that allow for control of one's learning?** *(Skill 4.1) (Average)*

   A. Humanistic

   B. Reconceptualist

   C. Behavioral

   D. Managerial

4. **Traditionalists are concerned with _____.** *(Skill 4.1) (Easy)*

   A. Selecting, organizing, and sequencing curriculum content

   B. Curriculum as an interactive system

   C. Curriculum as dialogue

   D. Curriculum as a child-centered endeavor

5. **Which of the following is a major assumption of the technical scientific approach?**
(Skill 4.1) (Rigorous)

   A. Curriculum development is dynamic and personal

   B. Curriculum development is subjective

   C. Curriculum development is rational

   D. Curriculum development is transactional

6. **Which statement <u>does not</u> describe the curriculum of an effective school?**
(Skill 4.1) (Average)

   A. The curriculum is planned with enough flexibility to address the changing needs of students

   B. The curriculum is planned a year at a time and encompasses basic skills that are learned in the classroom

   C. The curriculum is planned collaboratively with attention to basic skills and problem solving in the classroom and community

   D. The curriculum is planned with clear goals and objectives along with instruction activities and student assessment

7. **Which sequence best describes the order of a needs assessment?**
(Skill 4.2) (Rigorous)

   A. Survey of needs, goals and objectives development, problem identification, implementation planning, process evaluation

   B. Problem identification, survey of needs, goals and objectives development, implementation planning, process evaluation

   C. Problem identification, survey of needs, goals and objectives development, process evaluation, implementation planning

   D. Survey of needs, problem identification, goals and objectives development, implementation planning, process evaluation

8. Which of the following refers to the horizontal organization of the elements of the curriculum?
(Skill 4.2) (Rigorous)

A. The knowledge and skills that students learn are useful in life situations

B. The knowledge and skills that students learn at one grade level are relevant and useful as they progress to higher grades

C. Everything students learn contributes to fulfillment

D. What students learn in one class supports and reinforces what they learn in other classes

9. Which of the following refers to the vertical organization of the elements of the curriculum?
(Skill 4.2) (Average)

A. Everything that students learn contributes to fulfillment

B. The knowledge and skills that students learn at one grade level are relevant and useful as they progress to higher grades

C. What students learn in one class supports and reinforces what they learn in other classes

E. The knowledge and skills students learn are useful in life situations

10. _____ is based on the clustering of subjects into categories of study.
(Skill 4.2) (Easy)

A. Process-centered curriculum design

B. Subject-centered curriculum design

C. Discipline-centered curriculum design

D. Broad fields curriculum design

11. Which of the following statements best describes process evaluation?
(Skill 4.2) (Average)

A. It is concerned with the needs of the program

B. It is concerned with the adequacy of resources to implement the program

C. It is concerned with recording procedures and continuous monitoring

D. It is concerned with the attainment of the goals for the program

12. _____ is the type of evaluation that is concerned with how to utilize the resources to attain the goals of the program.
(Skill 4.2) (Easy)

A. Input evaluation

B. Content evaluation

C. Process evaluation

D. Product evaluation

13. _____ refers to the linking of all types of knowledge and experiences contained within a curriculum plan.
(Skill 4.2) (Easy)

A. Scope

B. Balance

C. Integration

D. Continuity

14. After identifying the curriculum phenomena, which sequence best represents the order of data gathering for program assessment?
(Skill 4.3) (Rigorous)

A. Reporting the information, collecting the information, organizing the information, recycling the information

B. Collecting the information, organizing the information, recycling the information, reporting the information

C. Collecting the information, reporting the information, recycling the information, organizing the information

D. Collecting the information, organizing the information, reporting the information, recycling the information

15. Which of the following best illustrates a behavioral objective?
(Skill 4.4) (Rigorous)

   A. Students will be able to solve multiplication word problems at the rate of one problem per minute with 80% accuracy

   B. Students will appreciate the originality of cultural music

   C. Ten percent of the students will comprehend the implications of good health and physical fitness

   D. By the year 2018, the literacy rate among all adults will increase to at least 90%

16. Which of the following best describes the purpose of student assessment?
(Skill 4.4) (Average)

   A. To analyze performance at various stages of goal attainment

   B. To appraise curriculum goals and objectives

   C. To determine outcome in terms of cost and achievement related to cost

   D. To analyze various alternatives or program options

17. Which statement best describes the Discrepancy Evaluation Model?
(Skill 4.4) (Average)

   A. Standards and performance are established for the old and new programs

   B. Standards and performance are normed

   C. Standards and performance are compared to determine differences

   D. Standards and performance differences are shared with parents and the community

18. Which choice best represents balance in the curriculum?
(Skill 4.7) (Rigorous)

   A. Equal time for each of the courses offered

   B. More time for reading and math because they are difficult subjects

   C. Concepts linked to continuity and integration

   D. Opportunities for the development of concepts and skills applied to real-life experiences

19. _____ increases achievement and interpersonal skills.
(Skill 5.2) (Easy)

A. Ability grouping

B. Cooperative grouping

C. Tracking

D. Homogeneous grouping

20. When using this type of computer program, students are tested and placed at the appropriate level. They then proceed through successive levels, mastering the content as they go. The program keeps track of students' progress. This type of program is known as:
(Skill 5.2) (Average)

A. Simulation

B. Tutorial

C. Drill and practice

D. Problem solving

21. Which of the following are best sources of curriculum?
(Skill 5.4) (Average)

A. Textbooks and bibliographies

B. Students and society

C. Teachers and administrators

D. Parents and community groups

22. The students at Cornwell Elementary School have consistently surpassed district and state achievement test levels. During the current year, the scores are in the lower quartile. The MOST appropriate action for the principal to take at the school site would be to:
(Skill 5.5) (Rigorous)

A. Meet with the parents to get their support

B. Call an emergency faculty meeting to decide what to do

C. Analyze test results to determine areas and patterns of poor performance by students

D. Get assistance from his or her district supervisor to implement programs that have worked elsewhere

23. Which of the following is included in the planning domain of the FPMS?
(Skill 5.5) (Easy)

A. Diagnosis

B. Effective use of time

C. Lesson development

D. Preparation for testing

24. Which of the following is the best formative assessment practice for students?
(Skill 5.5) (Average)

A. Provide a comprehensive multiple-choice test at the end of the chapter

B. Provide several teacher-made quizzes during the chapter

C. Provide guided practice during the unit

D. Provide a combination of test formats in the chapter test

25. Which of the following is an indicator of instructional organization and development?
(Skill 5.7) (Rigorous)

A. The teacher stops misconduct

B. The teacher discusses cause and effect and uses linking words to apply principles

C. The teacher emphasizes important points

D. The teacher recognizes responses, amplifies, and gives feedback

26. Which statement best describes effective classroom planning?
(Skill 5.7) (Rigorous)

A. The teacher begins by gathering instructional materials to give meaning to the goals and objectives

B. The teacher begins by gathering the best textbooks with sequential outlines to cover the subject matter

C. The teacher begins by setting up the evaluation system with quizzes and tests to assess learning at the end of the chapter

D. The teacher begins by specifying the instructional goals and objectives, followed by the strategies for learning

27. **Which theory group best represents a curriculum that emphasizes affective, rather than cognitive, outcomes?** *(Skill 5.7) (Average)*

    A. Behaviorism

    B. Observation learning

    C. Phenomenology

    D. Cognitive development

28. **The best way to improve a school through staff development activities is to:** *(Skill 6.1) (Average)*

    A. Obtain a nationally recognized authority on the topic determined by teachers

    B. Involve teachers in initiating, planning, implementing, and evaluating the program

    C. Have a few teachers set up the program

    D. Have the principal plan and let a few teachers review the plan

29. **Faculty are scheduled to report for the new school year in three weeks. The first week is designated for faculty development and setting up activities in classrooms and throughout the school. In deciding the agenda for the initial staff meeting, the principal should:** *(Skill 6.1) (Average)*

    A. Develop the agenda alone

    B. Ask the teachers what they want on the agenda

    C. Use the agenda from the previous year

    D. Work with the administrative team to develop the agenda

30. This theory of motivation is categorized as a cognitive process model of motivation. It is based on the concepts of valence (perceived positive or negative returns for working in an organization), instrumentality (perceived probability of return after performing at a given level of achievement), and expectancy (belief of an individual that a given level of activity will result in the identified level of goal achievement). Which of the following titles matches the theory?
(Skill 6.2) (Average)

A. Goal theory

B. Three factor theory

C. Expectancy theory

D. Need hierarchy theory

31. Change through professional growth and development is <u>least</u> supportive through: *(Skill 6.2) (Average)*

A. Intensive staff development over time

B. Single-day workshops with specific activities for the new program

C. Project meetings to adopt new materials to the realities of the school

D   Classroom assistance by resource personnel to assist with program implementation over time

32. Which of the following definitions correctly identifies self-efficacy theory?
(Skill 6.2) (Rigorous)

A. Success is the result of applying causal explanations regarding achievement efforts and influence on the effects of expectancies

B. A person's judgment about his or her ability to perform an activity at a specific level of performance

C. Success and failure are due to uncontrollable factors

D. Attaching logic to emotional reactions engenders pride and responsibility.

33. A method to assist participants in staff development activities to retain information and apply it in the classroom is _____.
(Skill 6.2) (Rigorous)

A. Role-play

B. Case study

C. Lecture

D. Active learning that uses all senses

34. The basic postulate of this theory of motivation is that intentions to achieve a goal form the primary motivating force behind work behavior. Select the theory that best conforms to this postulate.
(Skill 6.2) (Easy)

A. Goal theory

B. Feedback theory

C. Attribution theory

D. Controllability theory

35. Principal Jones wants her school to learn more about differentiated instruction. What is the least effective way she can provide the training teachers need to implement this change? *(Skill 6.3) (Average)*

A. Two one-hour sessions after school

B. Bringing in a consultant for an all-day training

C. Three half-day sessions with district trainers

D. None of the above

36. During the interview process, the principal may ask about the applicant's:
(Skill 6.4) (Easy)

   A. Reasons for applying for this job

   B. Mother's maiden name

   C. Ages of children

   D. Disabilities

37. What is the name of the system for teacher appraisal in Texas? (Skill 6.4) (Easy)

   A. Teacher Appraisal System

   B. Professional Development and Appraisal System

   C. TTAS

   D. Texas Teacher Education Assessment

38. If the applicant pool is small, the principal should
(Skill 6.4) (Average)

   A. Put a substitute in the classroom

   B. Advertise the position again

   C. Select the best person

   D. Recruit additional applicants although the application deadline has passed

39. Which of the following is the most appropriate topic to discuss during a teacher selection interview?
(Skill 6.4) (Average)

   A. Past performance evaluation

   B. Union membership status

   C. Husband's reason for Moving

   D. Reference letter item

40. In redesigning the performance appraisal system at your school, which of the following methods would you use?
(Skill 6.4) (Rigorous)

   A. Checklist

   B. Ranking

   C. Peer review

   D. A paper written by the teacher

41. The head coach asks the principal to hire an assistant coach for the girls' track team. The recommended individual has a teaching degree for English, but the master schedule requires the individual in this coaching position to teach biology. What must the principal consider when making a decision about this recommendation? *(Skill 6.4) (Rigorous)*

    A. Title IX law

    B. No Child Left Behind (NCLB) Act

    C. IDEA law

    D. FERPA law

42. The building-level principal should perform which of the following performance appraisal tasks? *(Skill 6.4) (Easy)*

    A. Develop appraisal criteria

    B. Design the appraisal process

    C. Conduct post-appraisal conferences

    D. Assess the appraisal system

43. An employee has been incompetent all year although you have followed all steps to help her. She has instituted a grievance against you of allegedly harassing her and claims that she is an excellent teacher, as demonstrated by her work at other schools. You have documented her work and realize she was under personal stress and did not perform well. What will be your recommendation for her employment next year? *(Skill 6.4) (Rigorous)*

    A. Terminate her

    B. Conduct a hearing before an impartial tribunal before a final decision

    C. Rehire her because she had problems

    D. Request her to take a leave of absence for the next year

44. In selecting instructional personnel, the principal is responsible for: *(Skill 6.4) (Easy)*

    A. Establishing a committee

    B. Initiating the process

    C. Determining the recommendations for employment

    D. All of the above

45. In selecting noninstructional personnel, the principal does not have to check:
(Skill 6.4) (Easy)

   A. Past job performance

   B. Fingerprints

   C. Statements from references given by applicant

   D. Educational attainment

46. Criteria to evaluate personnel in schools should include which of the following?
(Skill 6.5) (Average)

   A. How well the parents like the teacher

   B. How well the children like the teacher

   C. How well the other teachers relate to the teacher

   D. Test score gains by students

47. The human relations approach to administration accentuates developing and maintaining dynamic and harmonious relationships. Select the individual whose writings undergird this approach.
(Skill 6.6) (Rigorous)

   A.   Follett

   B.   Friedrick

   C.   Donmoyer

   D.   Zuckerman

48. How has today's education reform harmed school climate?
(Skill 6.6) (Rigorous)

   A. Teachers are competing against one another

   B. Curriculum is rigid and scripted

   C. Test scores are overemphasized and overanalyzed

   D. All of the above

ANSWER KEY: SUBTEST II – INSTRUCTIONAL LEADERSHIP

1. B	25. D
2. C	26. D
3. C	27. C
4. A	28. B
5. D	29. D
6. B	30. C
7. D	31. B
8. D	32. B
9. B	33. D
10. D	34. A
11. C	35. D
12. A	36. A
13. C	37. B
14. D	38. C
15. A	39. A
16. A	40. C
17. C	41. B
18. D	42. C
19. B	43. B
20. C	44. D
21. B	45. C
22. C	46. D
23. A	47. A
24. B	48. D

RIGOR TABLE: SUBTEST II – INSTRUCTIONAL LEADERSHIP

Easy	Average	Rigorous
24%	38%	38%
1, 12, 20, 23, 31, 32, 34, 36, 37, 42, 44, 45	4, 8, 9, 10, 13, 16, 17, 19, 21, 24, 26, 27, 28, 29, 30, 38, 39, 46	2, 3, 5, 6, 7, 11, 14, 15, 18, 22, 25, 33, 35, 40, 41, 43, 47, 48

SAMPLE TEST: SUBTEST III – ADMINISTRATIVE LEADERSHIP
Directions: Read each item and select the best response

1. **Which of the following statements is true of school accounting practices?**
(Skill 8.1) (Average)

   A. All purchases from internal funds must be authorized by the principal or a person designated by the principal

   B. The principal is the only person authorized to sign checks for the school checking account

   C. Principals can pre-sign checks that a designated administrator can use when the principal is unavailable

   D. Administrators must record, present, summarize, and interpret accurate records to preserve the school's owner equity

2. **General principles of school cost accounting require schools to use a(n) _____ basis for accounting.**
(Skill 8.1) (Easy)

   A. Single-entry

   B. Cash

   C. Consolidation

   D. Accrual

3. **Who regulates the use of internal school funds?**
(Skill 8.1) (Average)

   A. State Board of Education

   B. Local school board

   C. School site-based management team

   D. School principal

4. **Mr. Price, the principal at Wilson High School, wants to make preparation of the campus budget a more collaborative process. The first thing he should do is:**
(Skill 8.2) (Rigorous)

   A. Contact various stakeholders to gather information

   B. Form a Budget Committee with representatives from all stakeholder groups

   C. Articulate a vision statement that shows a relationship between the school's budget and its improvement goals

   D. Draft a budget that can be used as a basis for discussion, assuming it will be modified by input from stakeholders

5. **Which of the following statements about campus budget committees is correct?** *(Skill 8.2) (Average)*

   A. A budget committee should consist of the principal, faculty representatives, parents, and community leaders

   B. The principal should write a vision statement that clearly lists school goals that need funding

   C. The committee's first job should be to collect data that relates to school financial planning

   D. The principal should provide training for committee members and explain school statutes that affect the school's budget

6. **A school principal faced with inadequate funds to achieve school goals can:** *(Skill 8.3) (Rigorous)*

   A. Use discretionary funds to support the school's mission and vision

   B. Seek help from all stakeholders

   C. Approach the site-based management committee for help

   D. All of the above

7. **Mr. Blanchard has taken care to match the qualifications of new teachers he hires with school needs and district policies. However, by the end of the first semester, he has received numerous complaints about two of his new hires, and some community leaders have criticized him for the teachers he hired. From the information provided, what is a likely explanation for this criticism?** *(Skill 8.3) (Rigorous)*

   A. The new teachers did not buy into the school mission and vision

   B. Students dislike the school vision and have complained to their parents about how the new teachers promote it

   C. Mr. Blanchard inadequately communicated his actions to community stakeholders

   D. Mr. Blanchard's hiring process is inadequate for his staffing needs

8. **Which statement best describes how the role of principal has changed in recent years?**
   (Skill 7.1) (Rigorous)

   A. School leaders must be forceful and feel confident about decisions they make

   B. Management is less hierarchical, so a principal must be proactive and disburse information horizontally and vertically

   C. Once an effective means of communications is established, a principal should follow it for all types of communications

   D. Administrators should limit information because people lower in the organizational hierarchy require less information to do their job effectively

9. **The calculation of the base student allocation formula is best expressed by which of the following formulas?**
   (Skill 8.3) (Easy)

   A. The FTE plus program cost factor, times base student allocation, times district cost differential

   B. The weighted FTE times base student allocation, times district cost differential

   C. The FTE times weighted FTE, times base student differential

   D. The weighted FTE times program cost factor, times base student allocation, times district cost factor

10. **Which of the following best describes the purpose of budgeting?**
    (Skill 8.3) (Average)

    A. A yearly and periodic task to define and justify expenditure

    B. Financial plan to expend funds

    C. Continuous planning to put the educational goals into a financial plan

    D. A statement of anticipated revenues to operate the organization

11. _____ deals with the day to-day operation of the school.
(Skill 8.4) (Average)

A. Internal services fund

B. General fund

C. Debt services fund

D. Special revenue fund

12. The district financial officer shared information about a fund that could be used for specific types of expenditures. He made reference to _____.
(Skill 8.4) (Average)

A. A group of accounts

B. A sum of money

C. A cash balance

D. A ledger

13. The largest category of local funds to support education comes from _____.
(Skill 8.4) (Easy)

A. Motor vehicle licensing

B. Mobile home licensing

C. Ad valorem taxes

D. Lottery

14. At the end of the budget term a school district finds that there is an excess of assets over liability. Which of the following describes what the district has?
(Skill 8.4) (Average)

A. Revenues

B. Working capital

C. Owners' equity

D. Fund balance

15. Which of the following formulas best describes public school accounting?
(Skill 8.4) (Easy)

A. Assets = Liability + Owners' equity

B. Assets = Liability - Fund equity

C. Assets = Liability + Fund equity

D. Assets = Liability - Owners' equity

16. Which of the following is not a principle of school accounting?
(Skill 8.4) (Average)

   A. Revenues and expenditures are recorded as the transaction occurs

   B. An accrual basis is used for transactions

   C. A cash basis is used for transactions

   D. Revenues earned are recorded as assets, and expenditures are liabilities

17. Which of the following statements best describes zero based budgeting process?
(Skill 8.4) (Rigorous)

   A. It examines each item in relation to expected revenues

   B. It begins with empty accounts to then justify the continuation of the expenditure

   C. It begins with accounts for the past three years and looks at the history of spending to justify new expenditures

   D. It integrates long-range planning with the resources provided to meet specific needs

18. Which of the following statements best describes the incremental budgeting process?
(Skill 8.4) (Average)

   A. It integrates long-range planning with the resources provided to meet specific needs

   B. It begins with empty accounts to then justify the continuation of the expenditure

   C. It begins with accounts for the past three years and looks at the history of spending to justify new expenditures

   D. It examines each item in relation to expected revenues

19. Which of the following best describes the purpose of the evaluation component in the process of budgeting?
(Skill 8.4) (Average)

   A. To determine the attainment of goals, the effectiveness of cost and benefits, and new needs over a period of time

   B. To justify new expenditures and needed revenues

   C. To decrease or increase a line item in the budget

   D. To keep abreast of unit or program cost

20. The superintendent has requested a report on the science program at Middlebrook Middle School for use in submitting a proposal to the legislature via the Department of Education. She needs the material in a week. As principal, you have given the assignment to the chairperson of the science department and asked him to involve all appropriate staff and faculty members. You will monitor the progress of this activity by having the chairperson report to you at least daily and as deemed necessary by the chairperson. This monitoring system is: *(Skill 8.5) (Rigorous)*

A. Unnecessary meddling by the principal

B. An excellent delegation strategy

C. Time-consuming, but necessary to meet the superintendent's deadline

D. Important as an element in the management process

21. A school administrator has determined a number of tasks that must be completed during the course of the school year. They have been divided between two assistant principals, who are instructed to organize the tasks using a Gantt chart. A Gantt chart graphically displays the activities and the time frame for completing the activities. Which of the following statements best describes the advantage of using a Gantt chart for this planning process? *(Skill 8.5) (Rigorous)*

A. Using the Gantt Chart allows identification of the cause and effect associated with project completion or noncompletion

B. At any given point, the administrator can check on the progress of activities

C. The chart identifies the resources needed to complete a specific activity on time

D. The chart projects who and what programs need to be altered as the project nears completion

22. Who should report a problem in the restroom that concerns safety? *(Skill 9.1) (Easy)*

    A. A student should report it to the teacher

    B. The teacher should report it to the principal

    C. The principal should report it to the maintenance department

    D. All of the above

23. During the annual fire code inspection, the fire marshal wrote a violation for which of the following on an elementary campus? *(Skill 9.2) (Rigorous)*

    A. Bookcase was blocking a corridor

    B. Fire extinguishers were missing from several rooms

    C. Notes from latest fire drill indicated that building evacuation took too long

    D. None of the above

24. A principal wants to provide security training for the bus drivers. Which of the following would be a resource that could be used?
(Skill 9.3) (Average)

    A. Transportation supervisor

    B. Homeland Security

    C. Lead bus driver

    D. Local police department

23. The day-to-day operation of the school is regulated by mandates from _____.
(Skill 9.4) (Easy)

    A. the Commissioner of Education

    B. the federal government

    C. the state legislature

    D. the governor

ANSWER KEY: SUBTEST III – ADMINISTRATIVE LEADERSHIP

1. A	10. C	19. D
2. D	11. B	20. C
3. A	12. A	21. B
4. A	13. C	22. D
5. D	14. D	23. A
6. D	15. C	24. B
7. C	16. C	25. C
8. B	17. B	
9. B	18. A	

RIGOR TABLE: SUBTEST III – ADMINISTRATIVE LEADERSHIP

Easy	Average	Rigorous
24%	44%	32%
2, 9, 13, 15, 22, 25	1, 3, 5, 10, 11, 12, 14, 16, 18, 19, 24	4, 6, 7, 8, 17, 20, 21, 23

Rationales with Sample Questions

SUBTEST I – SCHOOL COMMUNITY LEADERSHIP
Directions: Read each item and select the best response.

1. The demographics have markedly changed over the past few years for the neighborhood from which the students at Jones High School come. The single-family homes are now occupied by multiple families. The first language of most adults has changed from English to Spanish. The businesses in the community are also changing and are requiring different types of skilled employees. You, as principal, have been asked to redesign your program to better meet the businesses' labor needs. Your first step to meet these need is to: *(Skill 1.2) (Average)*

    A. Talk to the new residents at a town meeting you establish at the school

    B. Conduct a survey of the business owners to determine their needs

    C. Plan to enlarge the school to meet increased student enrollment

    D. Discuss the matter with your area supervisor

Answer: B. Conduct a survey of the business owners to determine their needs
The first step in planning change is to conduct a needs assessment to determine the change needed.

2. What must become the norm for teachers to improve teaching and learning? *(Skill 1.3) (Rigorous)*

    A. Higher pay

    B. Time to work alone with their students

    C. Better training

    D. Time to plan with colleagues

Answer: D. Time to plan with colleagues
Quality teaching requires strong professional learning communities. Principals must provide time for collegial interchange, not isolation, for teaching and learning to improve.

3. Which area does a good education benefit most? *(Skill 1.4) (Average)*

A. Individuals enjoy a higher standard of living

B. Society has a skilled workforce that stimulates economic growth

C. Both A and B

D. Neither A nor B

Answer: C. Both A and B
Education is both a public and a private good because it enhances the individual as it benefits society (Swanson and King, 1997). At an individual level, education provides the ability to enjoy a higher standard of living by earning more money and living a better quality of life, thus making a contribution to the economy. Education supports the production of a skilled workforce for the efficient functioning of a society that is stimulated by economic growth and development.

7. What does a principal need before writing a strategic plan?
   (Skill 1.5) (Rigorous)

A. All necessary information

B. Identification of a problem or need

C. A commitment to action

D. None of the above

Answer: B. Identification of a problem or need
Planning needs to emerge from problems in the environment that are identified and defined. Planning is a commitment to think before acting. Planning, like decision making, often occurs without all the necessary information. Critics of the current drive for "strategic planning" argue that too much attention given to planning hinders school personnel from accomplishing their plans. However, no planning is worse than poor planning.

8. **Which of the following student achievement data should be used in formulating the school's strategic plan?** *(Skill 1.5) (Average)*

   A. STAAR test results

   B. District benchmarks

   C. Classroom assessments

   D. All of the above

Answer: D. All of the above
To gain a deeper understanding of students' learning needs, teachers need to collect and analyze data from multiple sources, such as annual state assessments, interim district and school assessments, classroom performance, and other relevant sources. Principals should look for school-wide trends and patterns in this data.

6. **Smith Elementary School is on the critically low list for the second year. About 90% of the students are on free and reduced lunches. Most live in the public housing project in single-parent homes. Strategies used last year did not significantly improve student achievement. To change this school, you would:** *(Skill 1.6) (Rigorous)*

   A. Have an initial session with a consultant and the teachers to determine how to proceed before developing a plan

   B. Seek to involve more parents in the education of their children

   C. Meet with the teachers and develop new strategies

   D. Form a small committee to establish what should be done

Answer: A. Have an initial session with a consultant and the teachers to determine how to proceed before developing a plan
It is important to include all stakeholders in the planning process for school improvement. Data should be reviewed to determine the great needs, followed by the creation of an action plan with specific goals, steps, and benchmarks to evaluate success.

7. **The state has put your school was put on the critically low school list. No measurable gains were recorded the second year, and you are on the list two consecutive years. How would you get your school off the list?**
    (Skill 1.6) (Average)

    A. Involve the community

    B. Have a meeting with teachers and establish a strategic plan that involves the parents and community

    C. Secure advice from the state and district and work on the problem

    D. Conduct a series of meetings with teachers, students, parents, and community members to obtain information in developing a plan of action with the faculty

Answer: D. Conduct a series of meetings with teachers, students, parents, and community members to obtain information in developing a plan of action with the faculty

This approach involves all stakeholders and will result in a plan of action that takes into account everyone's needs and suggestions.

8. **Recommended practice suggests that which of the following should be involved in the decision-making process concerning school improvement?**

    I. Teachers
    II. Community partners
    III. Administration
    IV. Parents and students
    (Skill 1.6) (Average)

    A. I and III only

    B. II and III only

    C. I, III, and IV only

    D. I, II, III, and IV

Answer: D. I, II, III, and IV

Strategic planning for school improvement should include all stakeholders. All parties should be represented in the identification of improvement goals and the plan to attain them.

9. **Which of the following best describes the process of school planning? (Skill 1.7) (Average)**

   A. The visionary principal, who knows about the needs of the school, develops the school plan

   B. Principal, teachers, parents, business partners, and other community members develop the school plan

   C. Principals, teachers, and parents develop the school plan

   D. A visionary team of teachers and administrators develop the school plan

Answer: B. Principal, teachers, parents, business partners, and other community members develop the school plan
A school plan needs input from all stakeholders. In a democratic process, everyone who is affected by the school has to have information about the budget, the programs, and the activities that are planned for the year. This ensures that all students get the best possible education. This process must also be ongoing so that it is continuously monitored and changed if necessary.

10. **Which of the following should mark the initial stages of school-based planning? (Skill 1.7) (Easy)**

    A. Developing a plan of action

    B. Evaluating the process

    C. Clarifying and articulating the mission and goals

    D. Analyzing the plan of action

Answer: C. Clarifying and articulating the mission and goals
Before any planning can take place, the stakeholders must identify their mission and goals. This sets out what they want to accomplish. The next step is to outline possible steps in accomplishing these goals.

9. A logical sequence in formulating goals is _____.
(Skill 1.7) (Average)

    A. philosophy, aims, goals, objectives

    B. philosophy, goals, aims, objectives

    C. aims, philosophy, objectives, goals

    D. philosophy, aims, objectives, goals

Answer: A. philosophy, aims, goals, objectives
The aims, objectives, and goals of the curriculum are derived from the underlying philosophy of education. Similarly, teachers develop aims, objectives, and goals for lessons based on their individual educational philosophies, which should be aligned with that of the school district and school. It is important to look at the philosophy to determine the objectives and goals for each subject. This is necessary in both horizontal and vertical organization of the curriculum.

12. Which of the following best illustrates an educational goal?
(Skill 1.7) (Average)

    A. Provide good health and physical fitness

    B. By the year 2018, the high school graduation rate will increase to at least 90%

    C. Develop self-realization

    D. The students will complete a reading comprehension examination within 30 minutes with 80% accuracy

Answer: B. By the year 2018, the high school graduation rate will increase to at least 90%
Every aspect of the curriculum is driven by goals. Goals are broad and take a long time to achieve, which is why they are further broken down into manageable outcomes. Goals must be specific and measurable. In this case, the parameters are set using the year 2000 and the graduation rate of 90%. When stakeholders examine the graduation results of students in 2000, they can compare them with the results of the year this goal was formed and determine whether the goal has been achieved.

13. Technological resources are limited in the school. The teacher in the Technology Lab does not want anyone else to use the equipment without her permission and supervision. Several teachers could operate the laboratory in an efficient manner. The best policy statement for the principal to make is to: *(Skill 1.8) (Rigorous)*

   A. Require the technology teacher to permit others to use the lab as long as they adhere to lab policies and meet the mission of the school

   B. Enforce the procedures established by the technology teacher

   C. Assign another teacher to the technology lab

   D. Get the teachers to reach an agreement

Answer: A. Require the technology teacher to permit others to use the lab as long as they adhere to lab policies and meet the mission of the school
Requiring all lab users to adhere to policy would be appropriate since the lab is a resource for all the school to utilize, as long as they follow the policy.

14. A teacher has asked the principal for funds to attend a conference on autism, the librarian has asked for additional library books, and the coach wants new football uniforms. How does a principal decide which request is approved? *(Skill 1.8) (Rigorous)*

   A. Look at the school improvement plan

   B. Seek guidance from the CPOC

   C. Allow the teaching staff to vote on the spending proposals

   D. Both A and B

Answer: D. Both A and B
Rather than making the spending decisions based on whim or favoritism, the principal should always be guided by the campus improvement plan and the Campus Performance Objective Council (CPOC). The CPOC is also known as the campus leadership team. As required by Texas Administrative Code, the CPOC will contain members representing the school staff, the parents, and the school community. For example, if funds are requested for an autism conference, but there are no school goals or student needs in this area, then this request should not be funded. If the school goals include literacy development, then a request for funding for additional library books may be approved.

15. During the induction process, the principal should ensure that the new teacher receives information about: *(Skill 1.9) (Easy)*

A. The school mission

B. Students who misbehave

C. Outdated policy handbooks

D. Parent attitudes

Answer: A. The school mission
The school mission is an important aspect since all activities within the school need to support the mission.

16. Student achievement scores have decreased. What is critical information that a principal must consider to improve student achievement? *(Skill 1.10) (Rigorous)*

A. Each teacher's results

B. Each student's results

C. What did not work

D. Both A and B

Answer: C. What did not work
Knowing what did not work helps the school find solutions that will raise student achievement. This cycle of data analysis, action planning, and assessment for results will lead to continuous improvement. Failure cannot be an option, and principals, as courageous leaders, must continually remind the school community that any setbacks are temporary.

17. **The principal of Bestever High School wants to create a Wall of Fame of photos of outstanding volunteers. This is an example of which principal competency?** *(Skill 1.11) (Average)*

   A. Acknowledge and celebrate the contributions of students, parents, and community members toward realization of the campus vision

   B. Support innovative thinking and risk taking within the school community

   C. Develop and implement strategies for effective internal and external communication

   D. Develop and implement a comprehensive program of community relations that effectively involves and informs multiple constituencies, including the media

Answer: A. Acknowledge and celebrate the contributions of students, parents, and community members toward realization of the campus vision
Creating a Wall of Fame honoring volunteers would be an example of acknowledging and celebrating the contributions of community members.

18. **Which of the following statements best describes the position method for studying community power structure?** *(Skill 2.1) (Rigorous)*

   A. Persons who hold the highest position in formal organizations are the community leaders

   B. Individuals who patronize the local population by distributing rewards and jobs are the community leaders

   C. Community leaders is based entirely on who has the most money

   D. Community leadership is based entirely on interlocking organizations and the relative power individuals can acquire as a member of numerous organizations

Answer: A. Persons who hold the highest position in formal organizations are the community leaders
In this method, consideration is given only to the traditionally recognized leaders in the community. An effort is made to determine those who lead community organizations and to build relationships with those leaders in an effort to build support for the school.

19. One method used in studying a community's power structure is comprised of the following steps. One, select several decision areas. Two, conduct in-depth interviews. Three, analyze documentary evidence. Identify this technique. *(Skill 2.1) (Easy)*

    A. Critical inquiry method

    B. Decision analysis technique

    C. Reputational technique

    D. Comparative analysis technique

Answer: B. Decision analysis technique
The decision analysis technique is based on the data collected during the interview process. The interviews are based on the decision areas that the committee has identified as important.

20. Mrs. Jones has just been appointed the new principal at the local high school. New to the area, she decides to conduct a community power structure study. First, she asks people knowledgeable of civic affairs to provide a list of individuals prominent in business, government, and civic affairs. Next, she asks a panel of persons knowledgeable about community affairs to select the most prominent of the leaders selected. Third, she interviews each of the individuals identified by the panel. Then, she analyzes the data to provide a view of the community power structure. Identify the technique used in her study of the community power structure. *(Skill 2.1) (Rigorous)*

    A. Comparative analysis technique

    B. Critical inquiry method

    C. Structured analysis model

    D. Reputational technique

Answer: D. Reputational technique
The reputation technique develops a list of community leaders based on the input of stakeholders in the community. This self-advocacy model creates a list of leaders from interviewing other leaders. It allows for the quick development of a list of leaders, but the list is limited because it is based on the preference of those interviewed.

21. **A type of community power structure is termed *amorphous*. Which of the following statements is an accurate description of this type of structure?**
    (Skill 2.1) (Rigorous)

    A. This power structure is characterized by a single group of individuals who make major decisions

    B. This power structure is characterized by multiple groups positioning for decision-making power

    C. This power structure is characterized by various groups from at least two communities having a common goal

    D. This power structure is characterized by an absence of a pattern of individuals or groups making decisions

Answer: D. This power structure is characterized by an absence of a pattern of individuals or groups making decisions

In the amorphous community power structure, decision making changes based on the decision being made and the parties involved. Rather than a codified process of decision making that is consistently used, there is no regular process. This may result in inconsistencies in the decisions that are made.

22. **Carver and Crowe summarized four basic community power structures as pyramidal or monolithic, caucus or factional, coalitional or polylithic, and amorphous. Which of the following statements best describes a factional or caucus power structure? (Skill 2.1) (Rigorous)**

    A. There is a relatively stable and predictable power structure

    B. Multiple groups and organizations elicit and impart power to the community based upon their interests

    C. Two or more groups vie for decision-making power

    D. Citizen input dominates decision making

Answer: C. Two or more groups vie for decision-making power

When two or more groups vie for decision-making power, the structures in place become even more important. If the administration supports and implements a codified system for making decisions, all parties involved can be assured of a fair and equitable process despite the groups struggling for power.

23. **Because schools are open systems and operate within a community environment, a school with an effective community relations program and a positive image may be more effective in:** *(Skill 2.1) (Easy)*

    A. Obtaining federal grants to support school programs

    B. Securing support from the community to carry out projects

    C. Being selected to appear on television programs

    D. Sending more of its graduates to college

Answer: B. Securing support from the community to carry out projects
An effective school and community relations plan is important for the success of any school. Relationships must be built with the community that engage community partners rather than just disseminate information to them. Such relationships increase support for the school and lead to community satisfaction.

24. **Which of the following statements best describes the competitive elite power structure?** *(Skill 2.1) (Average)*

    A. A group or groups of leaders who dominate community policies

    B. A group that is non-innovative and opposed to change

    C. A group concerned with ideological differences

    D. A group that embraces an open process of decision making

Answer: C. A group concerned with ideological differences
The leaders are usually embroiled in debates and disputes within the competitive elite structure.

25. **Which of the following statements best describes the monopolistic community power structure?** *(Skill 2.1) (Average)*

    A. A group or groups of leaders who dominate community policies

    B. A group that is non-innovative or opposed to change

    C. A group concerned with ideological differences

    D. A group that embraces an open process of decision making

Answer: A. A group or groups of leaders who dominate community policies
In the monopolistic community power structure, the word *community* refers to a small group of people with a monopoly over the organization.

26. Research on teacher participation in decision making reveals that teachers' involvement in formulating policies is an important factor in morale. The question that arises is: Under what conditions should subordinates be involved in decision-making? Which of the following statements best demonstrates an acceptable approach?
(Skill 2.2) (Average)

A. Apply the test of relevance, which asks if subordinates have a personal stake in decision outcomes, and the test of expertise, which asks if subordinates have the expertise to contribute to a decision

B. When it appears that the decision-making process will be victimized by the group-think syndrome, then invite subordinates to participate in the decision-making process

C. After preliminary consensus is reached, then invite subordinates to participate in the decision-making process

D. Once the decision-making cycle has been completed and the possible outcomes predicted, then involve subordinates in the decision-making process

Answer: A. Apply the tests of relevance, which asks if subordinates have a personal stake in decision outcomes, and the test of expertise, which asks if subordinates have the expertise to contribute to a decision
It is important to involve as many stakeholders in the decision-making process as possible. Consensus building and collaborative decision making as a model requires a great deal of time and training for all involved. It is important that those involved in the decision-making process have a vested interest in the policy or decision at hand.

26. The first step in using good group persuasive techniques is to: *(Skill 2.2) (Easy)*

   A. Plan an in-depth report of facts and statistics to support your argument

   B. Analyze the biases, emotions, and interests of the group to be addressed

   C. Make an impassioned, emotional appeal

   D. Solicit listener opinion before stating your objective

Answer: B. Analyze the biases, emotions, and interests of the group to be addressed
Analyzing the emotions, interests, and biases will allow you to prepare an argument that takes these into consideration, with stronger chances of persuasion.

28. The appropriate administrator completes the master plan of teaching assignments for the coming school year in time to notify teachers of their assignments before the current school year ends. This step will increase teacher morale: *(Skill 2.2) (Rigorous)*

   A. If the plan is published so they can make lesson-planning adjustments during the summer

   B. If its purpose is to solicit feedback to make changes satisfactory to most teachers

   C. Even if last-minute changes have to be made before school opens

   D. Because they know that the administration is acting in good faith

Answer: B. If its purpose is to solicit feedback to make changes satisfactory to most teachers
Soliciting teacher feedback will boost their morale because they will feel that they are an important part of the decision-making process and that their voices are heard.

29. You are a new principal in a school where 95% of the faculty has been on staff during your previous five-year tenure as assistant principal at the same site. Grapevine says that during faculty meetings you speak in half sentences and frequently make reference to events and situations with which only long-time teachers are familiar. You should: *(Skill 2.3) (Rigorous)*

A. Bring a larger group into your inner circle

B. Allow teachers to ask clarification questions

C. Continue to seek grapevine feedback

D. Speak to teachers about their problems decoding your presentations

Answer: B. Allow teachers to ask clarification questions
Allowing teachers to ask questions during the meeting will alleviate the concern that a few teachers may not know what you are referring to.

30. **Which of the following represents the proper sequence of the communication process?** *(Skill 2.3) (Easy)*

A. Ideating, decoding, transmitting, receiving, encoding, acting

B. Ideating, encoding, transmitting, receiving, decoding, acting

C. Ideating, transmitting, encoding, receiving, decoding, acting

D. Ideating, encoding, transmitting, receiving, acting, decoding

Answer: B. Ideating, encoding, transmitting, receiving, decoding, acting
These are the six steps of communication:
Ideating: development of idea or message to be communicated
Encoding: organization of idea into conveyable symbols
Transmitting: delivery of message through a medium
Receiving: claiming of message by receiver
Decoding: translation of message by receiver
Acting: Action taken by receiver in response to message.

31. Communication in which a school principal receives feedback from the faculty/staff is: *(Skill 2.4) (Average)*

A. Downward

B. Lateral

C. Upward

D. Diagonal

Answer: C. Upward
Upward communication is from personnel to a supervisor.

32. Which of the following is _not_ true of the educational grapevine? *(Skill 2.4) (Average)*

A. It is the least reliable source of transmitting information

B. It is the means by which most information is passed laterally among employees

C. Its most negative feature is the transmission of unsubstantiated rumor

D. It can be used effectively by administrators to test employee reactions that facilitate the decision-making process

Answer: A. It is the least reliable source of transmitting information
The educational grapevine is an important means of disseminating information. The grapevine should not be used for sensitive or confidential information, but it is an ideal system for quickly sending announcements to the entire staff. A grapevine should be developed early in the year and fully explained so that all staff is included.

33. Who needs to communicate well in a school? *(Skill 2.5) (Easy)*

    A. The principal

    B. The teachers

    C. The parents

    D. All of the above

Answer: D. All of the above

For proper operations, schools require good communication. Parents need to communicate information to teachers and other school staff members; students need to communicate to teachers and administrators; administrators need to communicate to parents, community members, students, and district leaders; and teachers need to communicate to students, parents, and administrators.

34. If a principal wants students to achieve higher grades and test scores, then he or she must provide: *(Skill 2.6) (Rigorous)*

    A. After-school tutorials

    B. Summer school

    C. Opportunities for parents to be involved

    D. Data analysis training

Answer: C. Opportunities for parents to be involved

Research has proven that when schools and parents work together, children receive higher grades and test scores. A key responsibility of the principal is to continually provide opportunities for parents/caregivers to be involved in the education of their children.

35. **Which of the following statements describes the responsibilities of today's principals?** *(Skill 3.1) (Easy)*

   A. A principal's behavior, stated communication, and implied communication have a tremendous impact on those around him or her

   B. A principal must resolve conflict in a systematic, fair manner and promote this behavior in others

   C. A principal is responsible for maintaining a positive perception of the school and must control negative information about all aspects of the school.

   D. All of the above

Answer: D. All of the above
Today's principals face new challenges. They must communicate effectively, manage diverse populations fairly and without bias, and create a positive perception for their school.

36. **Which of the following set of topics best describes the Revised Code of Ethics and Standard Practices for Texas Educators?** *(Skill 3.2) (Average)*

   A. Ethical guidelines for accepting gifts, record keeping, and professional relationships

   B. Confidentiality, misappropriation of funds, and litigation

   C. Personal conduct, conduct toward colleagues, and conduct toward students

   D. Political, fiscal, and ethical responsibilities

Answer: C. Personal conduct, conduct toward colleagues, and conduct toward students
The Revised Code of Ethics and Standard Practices for Texas Educators contains three parts:
I. Personal conduct
II. Conduct toward colleagues
III. Conduct toward students

37. **The Individuals with Disabilities Education Act (IDEA) was enacted to:** *(Skill 3.4) (Average)*

   A. Ensure students overcome language barriers that impede equal participation in instructional programs

   B. Provide equal educational opportunities for students, regardless of race, color, or national origin

   C. Improve accountability, expand services, simplify parental involvement, and provide earlier access to services and supports for students with special needs

   D. Ensure confidentiality of records and other information about students, parents, or staff members with disabilities

Answer: C. Improve accountability, expand services, simplify parental involvement, and provide earlier access to services and supports for students with special needs
IDEA specifically addresses the needs of individuals with disabilities. It does not focus on (A) language learning, (B) general equality of opportunity, or (D) confidentiality.

38. **Since participating in our democratic society is critical for the future of our country, what can Principal Martinez do to prepare students to be responsible, active citizens?** *(Skill 3.6) (Rigorous)*

   A. Choose a curriculum that emphasizes ethical principles, moral values, and civic participation

   B. Expose students to role models who have achieved success and personally demonstrate responsible behavior

   C. Promote the continuous and appropriate development of all students

   D. All of the above

Answer: D. All of the above
Principals must make every effort to prepare all students for participation in our democratic society. This includes using appropriate resources, presenting role models, and establishing an inclusive environment that encourages all students to participate.

39. Principals have a responsibility to act as _____ for the children they serve every day. *(Skill 3.7) (Easy)*

A. advocates

B. disciplinarians

C. teachers

D. coaches

Answer: A. advocates
An advocate is a person who speaks or writes in support or defense of a person or cause. Principals have a responsibility to act as advocates for the children they serve every day.

40. What should a principal who is new to a school do to promote necessary change? *(Skill 3.8) (Rigorous)*

A. Identify areas of need and thoroughly research new programs that could alleviate the problem

B. Spend a short time observing school procedures and make the most important changes immediately

C. Involve teachers and other stakeholders in the planning and development process

D. Impose ideas, because many teachers are afraid of change and will not cooperate unless an authority figure requires their participation

Answer: C. Involve teachers and other stakeholders in the planning and development process
School change is a difficult process. It is most likely to be effective when all stakeholders are involved in the process from the start. Importing new programs (A) is ineffective; trying to effect immediate change (B) doesn't work; and top-down management (D) is also ineffective.

41. Which of the following strategies is _least_ likely to cause students to embrace diversity? *(Skill 3.9) (Rigorous)*

    A. Provide opportunities for students to share their life experiences and cultures

    B. Strive to make all students and parents feel welcome and included in every aspect of the school community

    C. Depend on teachers and textbooks to provide an accurate and comprehensive global vision

    D. Build a school culture based on a foundation of respect and high expectations

Answer: C. Depend on teachers and textbooks to provide an accurate and comprehensive global vision
Diversity offers an opportunity for all students (and teachers) to learn about other cultures and customs first hand. A teacher's lectures and information in books is far less interesting and effective.

42. **Ms. Martinez teaches World Geography at a high school at which 60% of the students are Hispanic, 20% are African American, and 20% are European American. Which would be the best project for her to assign to start the school year if she wants to benefit from the diversity of her students?** *(Skill 3.9) (Rigorous)*

A. Give each student a map of the world on which to identify and color a list of countries; she will then display the maps

B. Have students work in homogeneous groups and compare the similarities and differences of their parents' families

C. Give an overview of the semester's objectives, assign the first chapter of the textbook, and have students work in groups to compare their answers to the questions at the end of the chapter

D. Have each student locate his or her family's country(ies) by placing a color-coded pin on a large world map; have students share a story about their family's coming to the United States with the entire class

Answer: D. Have each student locate his or her family's country(ies) by placing a color-coded pin on a large world map; have students share a story about their family's coming to the United States with the entire class
By having students locate their family's country of origin, the class would see the diverse parts of the world to which students had ties, and by sharing a story about how their family came to the United States, students would better understand diversity and their own family's unique contribution.

SAMPLE TEST: SUBTEST II – INSTRUCTIONAL LEADERSHIP
Directions: Read each item and select the best response.

1. _____ is the process of gathering information to identify and define the problem before initiating a project or program.
(Skill 4.1) (Easy)

   A. Surveying

   B. Needs assessment

   C. Evaluation

   D. Aims and goals identification

Answer: B. Needs assessment
Before initiating any project or program, it is important to determine what the problem is and the most effective solution. A needs assessment will help define the problem by collecting data so that an informed decision can be made as to the best way to start solving the problem. It is possible that what one deems to be a problem may not be the real problem the school needs to tackle.

2. **Effective teacher involvement in a new program is highly dependent on _____. (Skill 4.1) (Rigorous)**

   A. Teacher satisfaction with the curriculum planners' background

   B. District office politics concerning program planning and development

   C. Teacher involvement in the planning process and in-service training

   D. Parent and community buy-in to the design of the program and evaluation process

Answer: C. Teacher involvement in the planning process and in-service training
Teachers like to be involved in planning new programs and in determining the direction of the professional development. When new programs are introduced with teacher input, teachers are more likely to accept the programs and make them their own. When they can see how the in-service will improve their teaching and the students' learning, it will be easier to implement.

3. **Which of the following is an approach that sees the curriculum as emergent and concerned with cultivating the processes that allow for control of one's learning?**
(Skill 4.1) (Rigorous)

   A. Humanistic

   B. Reconceptualist

   C. Behavioral

   D. Managerial

Answer: C. Behavioral
The behavioral approach to curriculum offers a blueprint for teachers to use in their classrooms. It deals with setting goals and objectives and planning step-by-step lessons and activities that will help achieve these objectives.

4. **Traditionalists are concerned with _____.** *(Skill 4.1) (Average)*

   A. Selecting, organizing, and sequencing curriculum content

   B. Curriculum as an interactive system

   C. Curriculum as dialogue

   D. Curriculum as a child-centered endeavor

Answer: A. Selecting, organizing, and sequencing curriculum content
The two philosophies of education that are traditionalist are realism and idealism. Both stress an organized curriculum that proceeds in logical steps from one grade to another. In realism, the basic skills take top priority.

5. **Which of the following is a major assumption of the technical scientific approach?** *(Skill 4.1) (Rigorous)*

   A. Curriculum development is dynamic and personal

   B. Curriculum development is subjective

   C. Curriculum development is rational

   D. Curriculum development is transactional

Answer: D. Curriculum development is transactional
Transactional curriculum is process-oriented rather than problem-centered. The technical scientific approach allows learners to base assumptions on their transactions, or interactions with experiments and data.

6. **Which statement <u>does not</u> describe the curriculum of an effective school?** *(Skill 4.1) (Rigorous)*

   A. The curriculum is planned with enough flexibility to address the changing needs of students

   B. The curriculum is planned a year at a time and encompasses basic skills that are learned in the classroom

   C. The curriculum is planned collaboratively with attention to basic skills and problem solving in the classroom and community

   D. The curriculum is planned with clear goals and objectives along with instruction activities and student assessment

Answer: B. The curriculum is planned a year at a time and encompasses basic skills that are learned in the classroom
A, C, and D all describe what an effective curriculum should be. Answer choice B does not describe a curriculum that progresses naturally from one grade to another. It would result in a segmented curriculum in which the students would not graduate as well-rounded citizens.

7. **Which sequence best describes the order of a needs assessment? (Skill 4.2) (Rigorous)**

   A. Survey of needs, goals and objectives development, problem identification, implementation planning, process evaluation

   B. Problem identification, survey of needs, goals and objectives development, implementation planning, process evaluation

   C. Problem identification, survey of needs, goals and objectives development, process evaluation, implementation planning

   D. Survey of needs, problem identification, goals and objectives development, implementation planning, process evaluation

Answer: D. Survey of needs, problem identification, goals and objectives development, implementation planning, process evaluation

To determine what the problem is, the administrator, along with the teacher(s), should perform a needs assessment. This will help define the problem and lead to goal setting. To effectively solve the problem, there should be goals to ensure that pertinent information is gathered. Once this is done and the data is gathered, the stakeholders involved should determine which solution would be most effective and then plan how best to implement it.

8. **Which of the following refers to the horizontal organization of the elements of the curriculum?** *(Skill 4.2) (Average)*

   A. The knowledge and skills students learn are useful in life situations

   B. The knowledge and skills that students learn at one grade level are relevant and useful as they progress to higher grades

   C. Everything that students learn contributes to fulfillment

   D. What students learn in one class supports and reinforces what they learn in other classes

Answer: D. What students learn in one class supports and reinforces what they learn in other classes
Horizontal organization refers to making students aware of how the various subjects of the curriculum are interconnected. Teachers of different subject areas plan together so that they can teach and reinforce the same skills. Social studies and language arts courses are often grouped together. The social studies teacher not only ensures that students have the essential knowledge of the concepts, but also reinforces the writing and reading skills taught in language arts. Similarly, the language arts teacher can use books that reinforce the concepts of the social studies course.

9. **Which of the following refers to the vertical organization of the elements of the curriculum?** *(Skill 4.2) (Average)*

   A. Everything that students learn contributes to fulfillment

   B. The knowledge and skills that students learn at one grade level are relevant and useful as they progress to higher grades

   C. What students learn in one class supports and reinforces what they learn in other classes

   D. The knowledge and skills students learn are useful in life situations

Answer: B. The knowledge and skills that students learn at one grade level are relevant and useful as they progress to higher grades
Each area of the curriculum is designed so that the outcomes for one grade form the foundation for the learning that will take place in the next. Outcomes start out with the basics and build on them as students progress through the grade levels. If you look at a single outcome, you will see how it develops naturally as students are able to process more and more information. In mathematics, for example, an outcome for grade 8 may be that students are able to pictorially represent the square root of a number, and in grade 9, they are expected to solve problems using the square root of a number. This vertical organization of the curriculum ensures that students have the knowledge they need to be successful at each grade level.

10. _____ **is based on the clustering of subjects into categories of study.** *(Skill 4.2) (Average)*

   A. Process-centered curriculum design

   B. Subject-centered curriculum design

   C. Discipline-centered curriculum design

   D. Broad fields curriculum design

Answer: D. Broad fields curriculum design
In broad fields curriculum design, two or more subjects are blended into a broader field of study. Language arts, for example, combines the major communication skills of reading, writing, listening, speaking, viewing, and representing. The basis of using this curriculum design in elementary and middle schools is to avoid fragmenting the curriculum into separate subject areas. It also allows teachers to provide students with a greater integration of learning activities.

11. Which of the following statements best describes process evaluation?
(Skill 4.2) (Rigorous)

A. It is concerned with the needs of the program

B. It is concerned with the adequacy of resources to implement the program

C. It is concerned with recording procedures and continuous monitoring

D. It is concerned with the attainment of the goals for the program

Answer: C. It is concerned with recording procedures and continuous monitoring
Process evaluation is concerned with the implementation of curriculum. In the case of new curricula, it will look at the type of teacher professional development necessary for teachers to implement new ideas in their classrooms. Problems are dealt with as they occur, which means that there is continuous evaluation of the programs.

12. _____ is the type of evaluation that is concerned with how to utilize the resources to attain the goals of the program.
(Skill 4.2) (Easy)

A. Input evaluation

B. Content evaluation

C. Process evaluation

D. Product evaluation

Answer: A. Input evaluation
Input evaluation is concerned with getting the proper information to determine what resources are needed. It looks at whether the goals and objectives are suited to the program and whether they are stated properly. It also looks at whether the best resources are used, whether the strategies are appropriate, and whether any changes need to be made.

13. _____ refers to the linking of all types of knowledge and experiences contained within a curriculum plan.
(Skill 4.2) (Average)

    A. Scope

    B. Balance

    C. Integration

    D. Continuity

Answer: C. Integration
In an integrated curriculum, students are exposed to knowledge in several different subjects that are related to one another. The same concepts may be presented in different subjects in different ways. This type of curriculum organization brings together aspects of the broader areas of the curriculum into a meaningful whole. The teaching and learning reflects the real world with lessons and assessments that are cross-curricular.

14. After identifying the curriculum phenomena, which sequence best represents the order of data gathering for program assessment?
(Skill 4.3) (Rigorous)

    A. Reporting the information, collecting the information, organizing the information, recycling the information

    B. Collecting the information, organizing the information, recycling the information, reporting the information

    C. Collecting the information, reporting the information, recycling the information, organizing the information

    D. Collecting the information, organizing the information, reporting the information, recycling the information

Answer: D. Collecting the information, organizing the information, reporting the information, recycling the information
To identify and solve any problem, the first steps are to collect the data necessary and then to organize this information. Once the organization is complete, then those involved in the implementation or solution can report their findings to the stakeholders. Recycling the information is what you do with the results of the data collection. You may find an effective solution or find that only some of the information you have is relevant. You may have to start over if you decide that the information is not what you want.

**15. Which of the following best illustrates a behavioral objective?
(Skill 4.4) (Rigorous)**

A. Students will be able to solve multiplication word problems at the rate of one problem per minute with 80% accuracy

B. Students will appreciate the originality of cultural music

C. Ten percent of the students will comprehend the implications of good health and physical fitness

D. By the year 2018, the literacy rate among all adults will increase to at least 90%

Answer: A. Students will be able to solve multiplication word problems at the rate of one problem per minute with 80% accuracy
Objectives of lessons are stated in behavioral terms so that teachers know what kind of behavior they expect to see in student performance. This behavior will help determine whether the students have achieved the objectives. The main part of objectives is the verb, which is usually expressed in terms of what the student will be able to do at the end of the instruction. The verb is also based on Bloom's taxonomy, and the objective should be specific and measurable.

16. Which of the following best describes the purpose of student assessment? (Skill 4.4) (Average)

A. To analyze performance at various stages of goal attainment

B. To appraise curriculum goals and objectives

C. To determine outcome in terms of cost and achievement related to cost

D. To analyze various alternatives or program options

Answer: A. To analyze performance at various stages of goal attainment
Assessment at regular intervals is essential for both students and teachers. This testing can be formal or informal in that the teacher can keep a record of the marks or just make notes regarding how the students are doing. As students are assessed, the teacher can decide whether they are experiencing success or difficulty and how best to help them. Assessment guides instruction. While grading is a necessary element in schools, assessment and grading are different. Grading occurs at the end of assessment.

17. Which statement best describes the Discrepancy Evaluation Model?
   (Skill 4.4) (Average)

   A. Standards and performance are established for the old and new programs

   B. Standards and performance are normed

   C. Standards and performance are compared to determine differences

   D. Standards and performance differences are shared with parents and the community

Answer: C. Standards and performance are compared to determine differences
When assessments are closely aligned with the standards for the curriculum, you can see where there may be deficiencies or overlaps. The standards and performances for each level are determined, and then they are closely scrutinized to see if there are any gaps. The discrepancies in any curriculum are determined throughout all phases of the curriculum planning.

18. Which choice best represents balance in the curriculum?
   (Skill 4.7) (Rigorous)

   A. Equal time for each of the courses offered

   B. More time for reading and math because they are difficult subjects

   C. Concepts linked to continuity and integration

   D. Opportunities provided for the development of concepts and skills applied to real-life experiences

Answer: D. Opportunities provided for the development of concepts and skills applied to real-life experiences
When planning lessons, teachers should ensure that they allow the students time to explore the concepts on their own so that they can make sense of them as they apply to their own lives. Students may understand the concepts and even do well on a test, but they will not be able to apply them to real-life situations without having opportunities to do so. These opportunities can include such things as discussions in class, performing science experiments, and doing projects alone and in a group.

19. _____ increases achievement and interpersonal skills. *(Skill 5.2)* *(Average)*

A. Ability grouping

B. Cooperative grouping

C. Tracking

D. Homogeneous grouping

Answer: B. Cooperative grouping
When students of mixed abilities are grouped together, they can learn from one another. The students work together to accomplish tasks. These groups are not static and change throughout the year, giving the students chances to work with all their classmates.

20. When using this type of computer program, students are tested and placed at the appropriate level. They then proceed through successive levels, mastering the content as they go. The program keeps track of students' progress. This type of program is known as: *(Skill 5.2)* *(Easy)*

A. Simulation

B. Tutorial

C. Drill and practice

D. Problem solving

Answer: C. Drill and practice
This type of program is similar to worksheets on which the student has to get a certain percentage correct to proceed to the next level. It may be done in such a way that the students think it is a game, but with each level they practice until they get it right.

21. **Which of the following are best sources of curriculum?**
(Skill 5.4) (Average)

   A. Textbooks and bibliographies

   B. Students and society

   C. Teachers and administrators

   D. Parents and community groups

Answer: B. Students and society
Since the changes in society have a direct impact on what students need to learn in school, society is one of the best sources of the school curriculum. Since students are expected to stay in school, the curriculum should also be relevant to their needs and interests. Through discussions with students, parents, teachers, and others involved with the children, curriculum needs can be determined, as well as areas that are posing problems for the students and areas that need to be more challenging.

22. **The students at Cornwell Elementary School have consistently surpassed district and state achievement test levels. During the current year, the scores are in the lower quartile. The most appropriate action for the principal to take at the school site would be to:**
(Skill 5.5) (Rigorous)

   A. Meet with the parents to get their support

   B. Call an emergency faculty meeting to decide what to do

   C. Analyze test results to determine areas and patterns of poor performance by students

   D. Get assistance from his or her district supervisor to implement programs that have worked elsewhere

Answer: C. Analyze test results to determine areas and patterns of poor performance by students
Student assessment data should be used to identify targets for campus instructional improvement. Once targets for improvement are identified, a search for effective and research-based programs can be done.

23. **Which of the following is included in the planning domain of the FPMS?**
(Skill 5.5) (Easy)

A. Diagnosis

B. Effective use of time

C. Lesson development

D. Preparation for testing

Answer: A. Diagnosis
Diagnosis is the precursor to instruction, because teachers need to assess what students do and do not know. Then the diagnosis becomes the basis for the instructional planning.

24. **Which of the following is the best formative assessment practice for students?**
(Skill 5.5) (Average)

A. Provide a comprehensive multiple-choice test at the end of the chapter

B. Provide several teacher-made quizzes during the chapter

C. Provide guided practice during the unit

D. Provide a combination of test formats in the chapter test

Answer: B. Provide several teacher-made quizzes during the chapter
Formative assessment takes place during the process of teaching a lesson. It can be either formal or informal, with the teacher assigning marks or making simple notes in his or her grade book. The teacher also could make a note to the student, reminding him or her of mistakes to watch out for. On another occasion, the teacher may look for the same things to see whether the student has improved on the lesson. Formative assessment shows teachers how well the students have mastered the objectives set down for the lesson or unit. When teachers see that students are having difficulties, they can adjust the instruction accordingly.

25. **Which of the following is an indicator of instructional organization and development?**
(Skill 5.7) (Rigorous)

A. The teacher stops misconduct

B. The teacher discusses cause and effect and uses linking words to apply principles

C. The teacher emphasizes important points

D. The teacher recognizes responses, amplifies, and gives feedback

Answer: D. The teacher recognizes responses, amplifies, and gives feedback
When teachers design instruction for the students, they will be watching for responses from the students to show if they understand the concepts or need further instruction. The teacher will amplify the responses, meaning that he or she will expand on them to further explain and instruct. The feedback teachers give students about their responses will help them determine whether the responses are correct. It will also give them the feedback they need to proceed or to go back and make necessary corrections.

26. **Which statement best describes effective classroom planning?**
(Skill 5.7) (Average)

A. The teacher begins by gathering instructional materials to give meaning to the goals and objectives

B. The teacher begins by gathering the best textbooks with sequential outlines to cover the subject matter

C. The teacher begins by setting up the evaluation system with quizzes and tests to assess learning at the end of the chapter

D. The teacher begins by specifying the instructional goals and objectives, followed by the strategies for learning

Answer: D. The teacher begins by specifying the instructional goals and objectives, followed by the strategies for learning
All students need to know what they will learn in a unit of study and how they will be evaluated. The teacher should translate the instructional outcomes into "I can" statements and post them in the classroom. Then the students know exactly what is expected of them. When teachers use exemplars to show students what the expectations are for mastering the outcomes, the students are better prepared for success.

27. **Which theory group best represents a curriculum that emphasizes affective, rather than cognitive, outcomes?** *(Skill 5.7) (Average)*

   A. Behaviorism

   B. Observation learning

   C. Phenomenology

   D. Cognitive development

Answer: C. Phenomenology
The responsibility of schools is to produce students that are able to take their place in society as good citizens. The phenomenology theory, or humanistic psychology, emphasizes total learning, which means educating the whole person. Based on Maslov's theory, when we educate the whole child, we will have well-rounded and happy citizens who know how to act and work in society.

28. **The best way to improve a school through staff development activities is to:** *(Skill 6.1) (Average)*

   A. Obtain a nationally recognized authority on the topic determined by teachers

   B. Involve teachers in initiating, planning, implementing, and evaluating the program

   C. Have a few teachers set up the program

   D. Have the principal plan and let a few teachers review the plan

Answer: B. Involve teachers in initiating, planning, implementing, and evaluating the program
Involving more teachers in staff development planning and activities will increase accountability and feelings of ownership and promote success.

29. **Faculty are scheduled to report for the new school year in three weeks. The first week is designated for faculty development and setting up activities in classrooms and throughout the school. In deciding the agenda for the initial staff meeting, the principal should:**
(Skill 6.1) (Average)

A. Develop the agenda alone

B. Ask the teachers what they want on the agenda

C. Use the agenda from the previous year

D. Work with the administrative team to develop the agenda

Answer: D. Work with the administrative team to develop the agenda
Part of being an effective leader is to involve other people in planning and decision making. This improves accountability and is time effective.

30. **This theory of motivation is categorized as a cognitive process model of motivation. It is based on the concepts of valence (perceived positive or negative returns for working in a organization), instrumentality (perceived probability of return after performing at a given level of achievement), and expectancy (belief of an individual that a given level of activity will result in the identified level of goal achievement). Which of the following titles matches the theory?**
(Skill 6.2) (Average)

A. Goal theory

B. Three factor theory

C. Expectancy theory

D. Need hierarchy theory

Answer: C. Expectancy theory
The expectancy theory is the belief that an individual will act in a certain way based on the expectation that the act will be followed by a given outcome and on the attractiveness of a given outcome to the individual. The three subareas are effort, performance, and attractiveness.

31. Change through professional growth and development is <u>least</u> supportive through: *(Skill 6.2) (Easy)*

A. Intensive staff development over time

B. Single-day workshops with specific activities for the new program

C. Project meetings to adopt new materials to the realities of the school

D. Classroom assistance by resource personnel to assist with program implementation over time

Answer: B. Single-day workshops with specific activities for the new program

A single-day workshop will do very little to provide the professional support and development teachers need for new programs or ideas. The professional development needs to be continuous and monitored so that it can change as needed. Items A, C, and D should all be used in combination to provide the most support for the teachers.

32. Which of the following definitions correctly identifies self-efficacy theory? *(Skill 6.2) (Easy)*

A. Success is the result of applying causal explanations regarding achievement efforts and influence on the effects of expectancies

B. A person's judgment about his or her ability to perform an activity at a specific level of performance

C. Success and failure are due to uncontrollable factors

D. Attaching logic to emotional reactions engenders pride and responsibility

Answer: B. A person's judgment about his or her ability to perform an activity at a specific level of performance

A person's success in situations will depend on that person's belief in himself or herself. It is a person's perception of his or her ability to plan and take action to reach a particular goal.

33. A method to assist participants in staff development activities to retain information and apply it in the classroom is:
   (Skill 6.2) (Rigorous)

   A. Role-play

   B. Case study

   C. Lecture

   D. Active learning that uses all senses

Answer: D. Active learning that uses all senses
The more senses that are involved in the learning process, the better the information is retained and accessed.

34. The basic postulate of this theory of motivation is that intentions to achieve a goal form the primary motivating force behind work behavior. Select the theory that best conforms to this postulate.
   (Skill 6.2) (Easy)

   A. Goal theory

   B. Feedback theory

   C. Attribution theory

   D. Controllability theory

Answer: A. Goal theory
Goal theory revolves around the manner in which individuals determine their goals in achievement. There are three factors: achievement goals, perceived ability, and achievement behavior.

35. **Principal Jones wants her school to learn more about differentiated instruction. What is the least effective way she can provide the training teachers need to implement this change?** *(Skill 6.3) (Average)*

A. Two one-hour sessions after school

B. Bringing in a consultant for an all-day training

C. Three half-day sessions with district trainers

D. None of the above

Answer: D. None of the above
Significant research on professional development has concluded that among the worst ways of helping teachers learn new skills or knowledge is by putting them through "one-shot" sessions that focus on a particular strategy or technique for the classroom. It doesn't matter if the training is one to two hours or five to six hours. In either case, these sessions give teachers no reason to apply their new learning and do not take into account adult learning theory, which suggests that adults learn best when they have an immediate application to their learning.

36. **During the interview process, the principal may ask about the applicant's:** *(Skill 6.4) (Easy)*

A. Reasons for applying for this job

B. Mother's maiden name

C. Ages of children

D. Disabilities

Answer: A. Reasons for applying for this job
The principal may ask only about reasons for applying for the job. Answers B, C, and D are not appropriate topics.

37. **What is the name of the system for teacher appraisal in Texas?**
(Skill 6.4) (Easy)

A. Teacher Appraisal System

B. Professional Development and Appraisal System

C. TTAS

D. Texas Teacher Education Assessment

Answer: B. Professional Development and Appraisal System
The Professional Development and Appraisal System (PDAS) remains in place as the state's approved instrument for appraising its teachers and identifying areas that would benefit from staff development.

38. **If the applicant pool is small, the principal should: (Skill 6.4) (Average)**

A. Put a substitute in the classroom

B. Advertise the position again

C. Select the best person

D. Recruit additional applicants although the application deadline has passed

Answer: C. Select the best person
It is important to have a certified person in each classroom. If time does not allow for a continued search, the principal should hire the best candidate. The principal should provide a mentor and additional resources to help the teacher develop skills during his or her first year.

39. **Which of the following is the most appropriate topic to discuss during a teacher selection interview?**
(Skill 6.4) (Average)

A. Past performance evaluation

B. Union membership status

C. Husband's reason for moving

D. Reference letter item

Answer: A. Past performance evaluation
Past performance is most relevant to the current potential job.

40. In redesigning the performance appraisal system at your school, which of the following methods would you use?
(Skill 6.4) (Rigorous)

   A. Checklist

   B. Ranking

   C. Peer review

   D. A paper written by the teacher

Answer: C. Peer review
Peer review is an effective strategy for involving other people in the appraisal process, and it results in useful observations.

41. The head coach asks the principal to hire an assistant coach for the girls' track team. The recommended individual has a teaching degree for English, but the master schedule requires the individual in this coaching position to teach biology. What must the principal consider when making a decision about this recommendation?
(Skill 6.4) (Rigorous)

   A. Title IX law

   B. No Child Left Behind (NCLB) act

   C. IDEA law

   D. FERPA law

Answer: B. No Child Left Behind (NCLB) act
With No Child Left Behind and its emphasis on "highly qualified teachers," principals will have to abide by state and federal laws regarding certification levels and degrees. *All teachers teaching core subject academic areas are required to meet specific competency and educational requirements.* For example, all secondary subject-area teachers must have a degree in the subjects they will be teaching. The assistant coach would not be able to teach biology with an English degree.

42. **The building-level principal should perform which of the following performance appraisal tasks?**
(Skill 6.4) (Easy)

A. Develop appraisal criteria

B. Design the appraisal process

C. Conduct post-appraisal conferences

D. Assess the appraisal system

Answer: C. Conduct post-appraisal conferences
The principal is responsible for having a post-appraisal conference with all personnel to discuss the strengths and weaknesses revealed by the appraisal and to set professional goals and objectives for improvement.

43. **An employee has been incompetent all year, although you have followed all steps to help her. She has instituted a grievance against you of allegedly harassing her and claims that she is an excellent teacher as demonstrated by her work at other schools. You have documented her work and realize she was under personal stress and did not perform well. What will be your recommendation for her employment next year?**
(Skill 6.4) (Rigorous)

A. Terminate her

B. Conduct a hearing before an impartial tribunal before a final decision

C. Rehire her because she had problems

D. Request her to take a leave of absence for the next year

Answer: B. Conduct a hearing before an impartial tribunal before a final decision
This approach would be most fair for the teacher and would ensure that others are involved in the decision to rehire or dismiss her.

44. In selecting instructional personnel, the principal is responsible for:
(Skill 6.4) (Easy)

  A. Establishing a committee

  B. Initiating the process

  C. Determining the recommendations for employment

  D. All of the above

Answer: D. All of the above
The principal is responsible for all stages of hiring instructional personnel.

45. In selecting noninstructional personnel, the principal does not have to check:
(Skill 6.4) (Easy)

  A. Past job performance

  B. Fingerprints

  C. Statements from references given by applicant

  D. Educational attainment

Answer: C. Statements from references given by applicant
The principal may check references as necessary but is limited in the questions he or she may ask of the person providing the reference.

46. Criteria to evaluate personnel in schools should include which of the following?
(Skill 6.5) (Average)

  A. How well the parents like the teacher

  B. How well the children like the teacher

  C. How well the other teachers relate to the teacher

  D. Test score gains by students

Answer: D. Test score gains by students
Test scores of students are one objective measure of how well a teacher is performing.

47. The human relations approach to administration accentuates developing and maintaining dynamic and harmonious relationships. Select the individual whose writings undergird this approach.
(Skill 6.6) (Rigorous)

    A. Follett

    B. Friedrick

    C. Donmoyer

    D. Zuckerman

Answer: A. Follett
Mary Parker Follett believed in the idea of collaborative relationships. She emphasized that strength in relationships is built by sharing power with others and not over them. Through the sharing of power, the entire organization is improved by reciprocal relationships.

48. How has today's education reform harmed school climate?
(Skill 6.6) (Rigorous)

    A. Teachers are competing against one another

    B. Curriculum is rigid and scripted

    C. Test scores are overemphasized and overanalyzed

    D. All of the above

Answer: D. All of the above
Aspects of today's education reform that are harming school climate include: competition among teachers and schools that reduces collegiality; rigid, scripted curriculum materials that deskill teachers and diminish creativity; and misapplication and overanalysis of test scores. For example, many elementary schools across the country have eliminated recess to increase instructional time.

SAMPLE TEST: SUBTEST III – ADMINISTRATIVE LEADERSHIP
Directions: Read each item and select the best response.

1. **Which of the following statements is true of school accounting practices?**
   (Skill 8.1) (Average)

   A. All purchases from internal funds must be authorized by the principal or a person designated by the principal

   B. The principal is the only person authorized to sign checks for the school checking account

   C. Principals can pre-sign checks that a designated administrator can use when the principal is unavailable

   D. Administrators must record, present, summarize, and interpret accurate records to preserve the school's owner equity

Answer: A. All purchases from internal funds must be authorized by the principal or a person designated by the principal
Principals, or their designees, must authorize all purchases from internal funds. (B) Checks must be signed by two people; (C) principals should never pre-sign checks; (D) schools do not have owner equity—they are publicly owned by the taxpayers.

2. **General principles of school cost accounting require schools to use a(n) _____ basis for accounting.** *(Skill 8.1) (Easy)*

   A. Single-entry

   B. Cash

   C. Consolidation

   D. Accrual

Answer: D. Accrual
Schools use accrual accounting.

3. **Who regulates the use of internal school funds?**
   (Skill 8.1) (Average)

   A. State Board of Education

   B. Local school board

   C. School site-based management team

   D. School principal

Answer: A. State Board of Education
The State Board of Education sets rules for the use of internal school funds.

4. **Mr. Price, the principal at Wilson High School, wants to make preparation of the campus budget a more collaborative process. The first thing he should do is:**
   (Skill 8.2) (Rigorous)

   A. Contact various stakeholders to gather information

   B. Form a Budget Committee with representatives from all stakeholder groups

   C. Articulate a vision statement that shows a relationship between the school's budget and its improvement goals

   D. Draft a budget that can be used as a basis for discussion, assuming it will be modified by input from stakeholders

Answer: A. Contact various stakeholders to gather information
The steps in collaborative budgeting are: 1) gather information from stakeholders; 2) select a committee with representatives from each stakeholder group; 3) have the committee create a common vision; 4) train committee members, explain school budgetary statutes, and provide all necessary information; 5) present data and accept input; 6) create a budget; and 7) present the budget to the district.

5. **Which of the following statements about campus budget committees is correct?**
   (Skill 8.2) (Average)

   A. A budget committee should consist of the principal, faculty representatives, parents, and community leaders

   B. The principal should write a vision statement that clearly lists school goals that need funding

   C. The committee's first job should be to collect data that relates to school financial planning

   D. The principal should provide training for committee members and explain school statutes that affect the school's budget

Answer: D. The principal should provide training for committee members and explain school statutes that affect the school's budget
Choices A, B, and C are incorrect because (A) the committee should be made up of all stakeholders, including noncertified staff and students; (B) the committee should collaborate to write the vision statement; and (C) the principal should collect relevant data before forming the committee.

6. **A school principal faced with inadequate funds to achieve school goals can:**
   (Skill 8.3) (Rigorous)

   A. Use discretionary funds to support the school's mission and vision

   B. Seek help from all stakeholders

   C. Approach the site-based management committee for help

   D. All of the above

Answer: D. All of the above
All of these choices could contribute to procuring additional funding.

7. Mr. Blanchard has taken care to match the qualifications of new teachers he hires with school needs and district policies. However, by the end of the first semester, he has received numerous complaints about two of his new hires, and some community leaders have criticized him for the teachers he hired. From the information provided, what is a likely explanation for this criticism?
(Skill 8.3) (Rigorous)

   A. The new teachers did not buy into the school mission and vision

   B. Students dislike the school vision and have complained to their parents about how the new teachers promote it

   C. Mr. Blanchard inadequately communicated his actions to community stakeholders

   D. Mr. Blanchard's hiring process is inadequate for his staffing needs

Answer: C. Mr. Blanchard inadequately communicated his actions to community stakeholders
It is likely that Mr. Blanchard made his hiring decisions without communicating with stakeholders. Since all types of resources carry emotional and personal weight with school community members, forgetting the political elements of running a school often damages relationships. It's unlikely the new teachers were not on board (A) if Mr. Blanchard took care in hiring them to meet school needs; (B) students would not single out new teachers regarding the school vision if all teachers support it; and (D) according to the information given, Mr. Blanchard gave careful thought to his hiring process.

8. **Which statement best describes how the role of principal has changed in recent years?**
(Skill 7.1) (Average)

    A. School leaders must be forceful and feel confident about decisions they make

    B. Management is less hierarchical, so a principal must be proactive and disburse information horizontally and vertically

    C. Once an effective means of communications is established, a principal should follow it for all types of communications

    D. Administrators should limit information because people lower in the organizational hierarchy require less information to do their job effectively

Answer: B. Management is less hierarchical, so a principal must be proactive and disburse information horizontally and vertically
Today's principals operate in a less hierarchical, more collaborative environment in which large amounts of information must be shared with all levels of the school community. (A) School leaders have always needed to be forceful and confident in decision making; (C) communication methods vary by situation and purpose; (D) people on all levels in the organizational hierarchy require adequate information to avoid misinformation and to do their job effectively.

9. **The calculation of the base student allocation formula is best expressed in the following formula.**
(Skill 8.3) (Easy)

    A. The FTE plus program cost factor, times base student allocation, times district cost differential

    B. The weighted FTE times base student allocation, times district cost differential

    C. The FTE times weighted FTE, times base student allocation, times district cost differential

    D. The weighted FTE times program cost factor, times base student allocation, times district cost factor

Answer: B. The weighted FTE times base student allocation, times district cost differential
To arrive at the weighted FTE, you multiply the FTE by the program cost factor. Then you multiply this by the base student allocation and the district cost differential to arrive at the base student funding.

10. Which of the following best describes the purpose of budgeting?
(Skill 8.3) (Average)

    A. A yearly and periodic task to define and justify expenditure

    B. Financial plan to expend funds

    C. Continuous planning to put the educational goals into a financial plan

    D. A statement of anticipated revenues to operate the organization

Answer: C. Continuous planning to put the educational goals into a financial plan
The budget portrays the type of educational plan that the district wants to have in place for the students. The financial plans must be in place so that schools know how much funding they have for the teachers and students and the kinds of programs in which they can engage for the year.

11. _____ deals with the day-to-day operation of the school.
(Skill 8.4) (Average)

    A. Internal services fund

    B. General fund

    C. Debt services fund

    D. Special revenue fund

Answer: B. General fund
The general fund is the one of most importance to the school. It is the one that funds the programs, substitute teachers, and all the supplies needed for the school. It also takes care of the staff salaries.

12. The district financial officer shared information about a fund that could be used for specific types of expenditures. He made reference to _____. *(Skill 8.4) (Average)*

   A. A group of accounts

   B. A sum of money

   C. A cash balance

   D. A ledger

Answer: A. a group of accounts
The district budget consists of eight different types of accounts, some of which deal with the school and others of which deal with the district as a whole.

13. The largest category of local funds to support education comes from _____. *(Skill 8.4) (Easy)*

   A. Motor vehicle licensing

   B. Mobile home licensing

   C. Ad valorem taxes

   D. Lottery

Answer: C. Ad valorem taxes
Ad valorem taxes are those levied on real estate and personal property. Since the amount of property tax helps determine the weighted FTE, they are important to schools.

14. At the end of the budget term a school district finds that there is an excess of assets over liability. Which of the following describes what the district has?
(Skill 8.4) (Average)

A. Revenues

B. Working capital

C. Owners' equity

D. Fund balance

Answer: D. Fund balance
The monies that remain in the budget are a balance. Since it is a school fund, it is called a fund balance.

15. Which of the following formulas best describes public school accounting?
(Skill 8.4) (Easy)

A. Assets = Liability + Owners' equity

B. Assets = Liability - Fund equity

C. Assets = Liability + Fund equity

D. Assets = Liability - Owners' equity

Answer: C. Assets = Liability + Fund equity
The assets are the funds that the school has access to and can spend. Liabilities are the expenses, and the fund equity refers to the reserves. Therefore, when you subtract the liabilities from the fund equity, this is the balance you have remaining in the budget.

16. **Which of the following is not a principle of school accounting?**
   (Skill 8.4) (Average)

   A. Revenues and expenditures are recorded as the transaction occurs

   B. An accrual basis is used for transactions

   C. A cash basis is used for transactions

   D. Revenues earned are recorded as assets, and expenditures are liabilities

Answer: C. A cash basis is used for transactions
Cash is never used as payment for anything that is paid for from the school budget. Checks leave a paper trail, which makes it easier to reconcile bank statements and to perform audits.

17. **Which of the following statements best describes zero based budgeting process?**
   (Skill 8.4) (Rigorous)

   A. It examines each item in relation to expected revenues

   B. It begins with empty accounts to then justify the continuation of the expenditure

   C. It begins with accounts for the past three years and looks at the history of spending to justify new expenditures

   D. It integrates long-range planning with the resources provided to meet specific needs

Answer: B. It begins with empty accounts to then justify the continuation of the expenditure
This process starts out with no money and then adds expenditures and revenues. In this manner, those involved in the budgetary process can make sure that the money is raised in a proper way and is spent as it should be.

18. **Which of the following statements best describes the incremental budgeting process?**
   (Skill 8.4) (Average)

   A. It integrates long-range planning with the resources provided to meet specific needs

   B. It begins with empty accounts to then justify the continuation of the expenditure

   C. It begins with accounts for the past three years and looks at the history of spending to justify new expenditures

   D. It examines each item in relation to expected revenues

Answer: A. It integrates long-range planning with the resources provided to meet specific needs

Incremental budgeting looks at the long term—two or more years—based on projected enrolments in the school. This gives the stakeholders the information they need to plan for activities that might extend over several years.

19. **Which of the following best describes the purpose of the evaluation component in the process of budgeting?**
   (Skill 8.4) (Average)

   A. To determine the attainment of goals, the effectiveness of cost and benefits, and new needs over a period of time

   B. To justify new expenditures and needed revenues

   C. To decrease or increase a line item in the budget

   D. To keep abreast of unit or program cost

Answer: D. To keep abreast of unit or program cost

Evaluation is necessary in budget planning to ensure not only that the money is being spent properly, but also that the school is not overspending.

20. The superintendent has requested a report on the science program at Middlebrook Middle School for use in submitting a proposal to the legislature via the Department of Education. She needs the material in a week. As principal, you have given the assignment to the chairperson of the science department and asked him to involve all appropriate staff and faculty members. You will monitor the progress of this activity by having the chairperson report to you at least daily and as deemed necessary by the chairperson. This monitoring system is: *(Skill 8.5) (Rigorous)*

A. Unnecessary meddling by the principal

B. An excellent delegation strategy

C. Time-consuming, but necessary to meet the superintendent's deadline

D. Important as an element in the management process

Answer: C. Time-consuming, but necessary to meet the superintendent's deadline
Even though the principal has delegated the task, regular supervision and feedback are important to ensure that the job is being completed.

21. A school administrator has determined a number of tasks that must be completed during the course of the school year. The tasks have been divided between two assistant principals. The assistant principals are instructed to organize the tasks using a Gantt chart. A Gantt chart graphically displays the activities and the time frame in which the activities are to be completed. Which of the following statements best describes the advantage of using a Gantt chart for this planning process?
(Skill 8.5) (Rigorous)

A. Using the Gantt chart allows the administrator to identify the cause and effect associated with project completion or noncompletion

B. At any given point, the administrator can check on the progress of activities

C. The chart identifies the resources needed to complete a specific activity on time

D. The Gantt chart projects who and what potential programs need to be altered or changed as the project nears completion

Answer: B. At any given point, the administrator can check on the progress of activities
Using a Gantt chart will give the principal a quick visual update on the progress of the project so that he or she can make informed decisions.

22. Who should report a problem in the restroom that concerns safety?
(Skill 9.1) (Easy)

A. A student should report it to the teacher

B. The teacher should report it to the principal

C. The principal should report it to the maintenance department

D. All of the above

Answer: D. All of the above
School leaders are charged with providing students a safe, efficient, comfortable school building, conducive to rigorous academic learning. A principal—or a designee, such as an assistant principal—should be responsible for making daily rounds on a campus looking for safety concerns. In addition, staff and students must help identify problems as they occur so that the principal can find a way to correct them.

23. During the annual fire code inspection, the fire marshal wrote a violation for which of the following on an elementary campus? *(Skill 9.2) (Rigorous)*

 A. Bookcase was blocking a corridor

 B. Fire extinguishers were missing from several rooms

 C. Notes from latest fire drill indicated that building evacuation took too long

 D. None of the above

Answer: A. Bookcase was blocking a corridor
Fire code does not require a fire extinguisher in every room. Although monthly fire drills are required, there is not a time standard for evacuating a building. Furniture that gets in the way of door areas/exits must be moved.

24. A principal wants to provide security training for the bus drivers. Which of the following would be a resource that could be used? *(Skill 9.3) (Average)*

 A. Transportation supervisor

 B. Homeland Security

 C. Lead bus driver

 D. Local police department

Answer: B. Homeland Security
To enhance school safety, the Department of Homeland Security offers funding, training, and resources, such as providing money for emergency preparedness, training school bus drivers in security, and hardening school buildings' vulnerability.

26. The day-to-day operation of the school is regulated by mandates from

_____.

(Skill 9.4) (Easy)

A. the Commissioner of Education

B. the federal government

C. the state legislature

D. the governor

Answer: C. the state legislature

Since the state is the body that directs the funding and the curriculum of the schools, it also mandates the day-to-day operation of the schools. The state has a legal obligation to direct how schools operate.

\ information can be obtained
\ICGtesting.com
\ the USA
\ 2122180618
\ V00011B/501/P